To Joanne

Happy a

Dorothy Ovler

Feb 93

· MEREHURST ·
EMBROIDERY SKILLS

QUILTING

· MEREHURST ·
EMBROIDERY SKILLS

QUILTING

Dorothy Osler

MEREHURST
LONDON

Published 1991 by Merehurst Limited
Ferry House,
51-57 Lacy Road,
Putney, London SW15 1PR

Reprinted 1992

A catalogue record for this book is
available from the British Library.

Project editor: Polly Boyd
Edited by Diana Brinton
Australian Consultant: Margaret Rolfe
UK Consultant: Annlee Landman
Designed by Bill Mason
Photography by Stewart Grant (except pages 6, 39, 52 (top),
59, 60, 61, 71, 77, 84, 85, 105, 117, 121, 124, 125)
Diagrams by Lindsay Blow
Typeset by
Rowland Phototypesetting Limited,
Bury St Edmunds, Suffolk
Colour Separation by
Fotographics Limited,
UK–Hong Kong
Printed in Italy by
New Interlitho S.p.a., Milan

CONTENTS

INTRODUCTION

Quilting is a centuries-old form of stitchery that has been newly invigorated and rejuvenated by its elevation and acceptance as a textile art form. Exciting and challenging, contemporary quilts and quilting ideas now complement the enduring traditional designs, patterns and techniques that have evolved over the years in many different countries and cultures.

In essence, quilting combines layers of fabric with, usually, some form of padding in between. The resulting softly sculptured surface has a visual and tactile quality with an age-old appeal, but it can also have a practical insulating purpose. For this reason, quilting – together with the associated crafts of patchwork and appliqué – has long been used for making warm bed covers, and the term quilting is much used to describe quiltmaking in its broadest sense. This book, however, is chiefly concerned with quilting as line stitchery through layers.

The basic techniques of quilting are simple in concept, but the real and satisfying demands of the craft lie in using pattern and space to give a rich textural quality – a quality which is further accentuated by the interplay of light and shade on the quilted surface. The experienced quilter knows how to exploit the subtle nature of the craft, but beginners or the less experienced can learn much by studying quilts, old and new, and judging how the variety and disposition of patterns used creates textural variation on the surface. In simple terms, this is a matter of noticing the way in which densely quilted areas apparently recede, while more open or unquilted areas stand out in relief, and the relationship between quilting design and other surface decoration. But don't count the stitches – as long as they are even and straight, the number to the centimetre (or inch) is not so important.

Quilting in the past

Quilting has a long history, but that history is obscured by myth and romanticism. What does seem clear is that quilting techniques were well established in the countries of the Middle and Far East before arriving in Europe in the Middle Ages. By the end of the 16th century, European quilting was in the hands of professionals, who produced quilts and quilted garments in costly fabrics such as silk and satin for use by the rich and powerful, and in woollen homespun fabrics for warmth and protection.

The expansion of trade with the Far East in the 17th century, however, provided a source of colourful, washable textiles that were

Left: *The detail of this 18th-century linen binder reveals exquisite cord quilting, in both back stitch and running stitch, together with openwork and french knot embroidery. (Photograph courtesy of the Tyne and Wear Museum Service.)*

Right: *Mrs Dorothy Gourd (1850–1923) of Chester-le-Street, County Durham, made this* Diamond in the Square *quilt in the early 20th century. The sawtooth borders in this detail suggest an American influence on the pieced design, and Mrs Gourd had strong family connections in America. Her quilting design is, however, characteristic Durham quilting.*

sensationally new to Europeans. Indian chintzes and palampores became hugely popular for quilts, which was not surprising, considering that only monochrome fabrics had been readily available until then.

As the stately East India ships sailed east, humbler vessels hurried west across the Atlantic carrying colonists to the New World. Among their homely possessions were quilts and quilted clothes, and among their skills was the knowledge of how to make such things. In the colonies of North America, quilt-making became a symbol of cultural togetherness and enduring creative expression.

In both the Old and the New Worlds, the 19th century was the period when quilt-making reached its peak. An extraordinary diversity of quilts were stitched, many of which survive to give a lasting legacy of colour, design and pattern. It was also in the 19th century that quilting developed a regional or cultural distinctiveness. The characteristic colours and patterns of Welsh and North Country quilts in Britain and of the Amish and Mennonite quilts of America, for example, are rooted in 19th-century quilt-making.

The 20th century has been one of mixed fortunes. Declining interest in the early years preceded a brief revival in the 1930s; failing interest after World War II was followed by the explosion of activity which has taken place since the early 1970s.

Quilting today

Freed from the functional constraints of utility or room decoration, quilts and quilting have evolved into a form of artistic expression which has its exponents in every part of the world. Freedom, too, from the symmetrical constraints of traditional quilts has allowed quilters to develop a variety of forms in which to express both their individuality and the stylistic fashions of the time. The unique subtleties of quilting itself and their contribution to the decorative quilt surface are now receiving more attention and evaluation than in the early years of the quilt revival. Traditional quilts remain a source of fascination and inspiration that has been expanded to embrace a whole new range of creative ideas.

Returning to her home in England after a visit to Australia, Annette Claxton synthesized her antipodean images into this vibrant quilt Down Under, *pieced in cotton fabrics and quilted with a design based on a tile pattern in Sydney Opera House. Size: 152cm × 152cm (62in × 62in).*

CHAPTER 1

MATERIALS AND BASIC TECHNIQUES

Fabrics for quilting

For quilting, fabrics need to be sufficiently soft and pliable to be stitched through without difficulty, particularly if the quilt is to be hand stitched. They must also be closely woven so that fibres of the filling will not work their way through, a problem known as 'bearding'. Soft cotton fabrics are most suitable for the beginner, but silk, linen, fine wool and some lightweight furnishing cottons are among other natural-fibre fabrics that are widely used. Some cotton/polyester mixes, such as poplin, quilt well, but on the whole fabrics with synthetic fibres are less pliable and harsher than those made from natural fibres.

Both printed and solid-colour fabrics – known as prints and solids – can be used. Fabrics with a sheen, from shiny satin to a mercerized cotton, can emphasize the textural quality of a quilt because of the way in which light reflects from a polished surface. Contrary to what you might think, it is not essential to wash fabrics before quilting unless you are piecing an intricate top; indeed the appeal of hand-stitched cotton quilts is sometimes enhanced after washing, when the fabric 'gathers' around the stitches.

The method that you intend using to mark out the design on the fabric and the long-term care of the quilt will affect your choice of fabric. Some marked lines can be removed only by soaking in water or by washing, and any quilt will need to be cleaned at least once and perhaps many times in its lifetime. Though cotton quilts can be washed, silk and woollen fabrics are best dry-cleaned, and no quilt should be pressed after washing or cleaning. (It is vital to emphasize this if you take a quilt to be cleaned.) Most specialist quilt stores stock a wide variety of fabrics, many of which are manufactured for the quilter, but it is well worth experimenting with other fabrics.

Suitable fabrics for quilting include (clockwise from top left) printed cotton lawn, crêpe de chine, cotton print, silk, fine wool, plain cotton, cotton poplin, plain cotton lawn, polished cotton, and cotton sateen, together with printed chintz and a matching cotton (centre).

Filling materials

The filling material for a quilt is known as batting or wadding. It is this which gives a quilt its particular character, rising up in relief in the unstitched areas; the amount of rise is known as 'loft'. Both natural fibre and synthetic fillings are available, but they have different properties which affect the finished quilt, so you must consider the character of your quilt before making a choice.

Polyester   Polyester batting is available in a variety of weights. In practice, a 56g (2oz) weight is most suitable for hand quilting; the heavier 75g (3oz) and 110g (4oz) weights can be used for machine quilting. Readily available in a variety of widths (up to a king-size bed width), washable and inexpensive, it is an ideal choice for beginners. The batting sold as 56g (2oz) weight can vary from place to place; ideally, it should be about 1.5cm (½in) thick.

Polyester battings vary in quality as well as in weight; those with soft fibres are preferable to the coarser varieties available from non-specialist sources. Some are springier than others and so give a greater degree of loft. 'Bearding', which is the movement of fibres through the surface of the quilt, can be overcome by choosing a bonded polyester batting. Large areas can be left unquilted if a polyester batting has been used because there is little movement after washing – a factor to bear in mind when planning a design.

In some countries, polyester battings have to be fire-retardant to comply with regulations: this affects both the quality and the variety of synthetic battings available.

Cotton   Manufactured cotton battings are available in a refined and unrefined form. Both are washable, but will move and shrink. Widths may need to be joined (butt-jointed) for large quilts. Unrefined cotton batting contains seeds that hinder stitching, as does the skin on some battings. The cotton types have less loft than polyester, but they also have a softer feel and a more fluid quality.

Cotton/polyester   The increasingly popular 80 per cent cotton/20 per cent polyester batting combines the softer feel of cotton with the evenness and loft of polyester and, having been produced especially for the quilter, is available in wide widths. It shrinks with washing, so it is often wise to pre-shrink it in hot water before use.

Wool Wool is soft, lightweight and warm. Wool battings suffer from bearding, though this can be overcome by adding a layer of lightweight muslin to the top surface. Wool also moves and must therefore be closely quilted. In many countries it is difficult to obtain, but in some, including Australia, it is widely available, either in pure wool form or in a wool/polyester mix.

Silk Silk batting is expensive but very soft, a pleasure to quilt and particularly suitable for use with silk fabrics.

Fillings for cord and stuffed quilting Cotton or wool yarns, of chosen thickness, are used for cord quilting; for stuffed quilting, any of the commercially produced battings can be eased apart and used.

Some examples of suitable batting (clockwise from top left): 110g (4oz) and 56g (2oz) polyester, heavy, medium and lightweight silk, refined and unrefined cotton, and wool for cord quilting.

Threads

For hand quilting, use quilting thread – dressmakers' threads are not strong enough. Quilting threads in a variety of colours are manufactured in pure cotton as well as cotton/polyester mixes. Other suitable threads include fine crochet cotton, linen thread and some embroidery threads. For quilting on silk, use silk thread. If you wax your thread by running it through a block of beeswax, this will help to ease it through the fabric layers.

For machine quilting, choose a thread appropriate to the type of stitch and fabric used. Some quilting threads can be used for straight stitching, but if you are using decorative stitches a finer cotton or silk

For hand quilting, a variety of cotton, silk and synthetic threads can be used; waxing helps to ease the thread through fabric layers. Thimbles of many different types are available for finger protection; choose one that you find comfortable to work with.

thread is more appropriate. Contemporary ideas include using transparent, variegated and metallic threads for machine quilting, and the range of these decorative threads is growing rapidly.

Needles and pins

'Between' needles are used for most hand quilting. For general purposes you will find a no. 8 the most convenient size, but the finer 10–12 sizes are better for stitching through fine fabrics and lightweight fillings.

For machine quilting, choose a needle size appropriate to the fabric – size 90(14) for dressweight and fine furnishing cottons or for wool, but size 80(12) for fine cottons or silk. A 4mm twin needle can be used for cord quilting.

Pins need to be long and fine. Those with glass or plastic heads are ideal, being easier to manipulate through quilt layers than standard dressmaking pins. They are available up to 5cm (2in) in length. When layering a quilt, especially one that is to be machined, you can use safety pins instead of basting stitches, but their relatively thick stems leave holes in fine fabrics. Try, if possible, to place safety pins within any pieced seams on the quilt surface.

Thimbles and finger protectors

Hand quilters always look at other quilters' fingers! Unless you wear some form of protection, pricked fingers are an inevitable result of hand quilting. The fingers most likely to need protection are the middle fingers of both hands and the thumb of your quilting hand. Thimbles provide good protection on the quilting hand, but the hand below the work may need something more pliable which will allow you to feel the needle coming through the layers. A variety of leather and plastic protectors are available for this purpose, though you can adapt something simple to suit yourself.

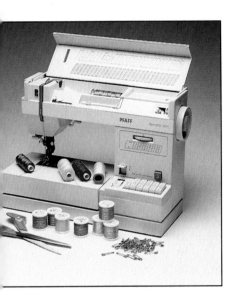

For machine quilting, the choice of threads is very wide. As well as threads spun from natural fibres, there is an increasing range of metallic and rayon threads, and these are growing in popularity.

Frames and hoops

For hand quilting, it is advisable to have some means of holding the fabric layers in place. The choice is wide, ranging from large frames to small hoops; each has its advantages and disadvantages, so consider these, and your individual needs.

Quilt frames

A large quilt frame is the ideal tool for holding the layers of a quilt during hand quilting. The layers do not need to be basted together before they are set in the frame; the work is handled less, and it is not crushed as it would be in the confines of a hoop or similar device. But a large quilt frame takes up a lot of space and is not easily portable. It also takes up a great deal of space when not in use; a traditional answer to the problem was to hoist the frame to the ceiling.

Large frames have four members – two long rails and two shorter stretchers. The rails need to be long enough to allow one full edge of the quilt to be attached. The 'traditional' frame is no more than four pieces of timber with webbing along the rails to which the quilt is attached, a slot through the rails to take the stretchers, and holes drilled in the stretchers for pegs to keep the frame in position. It has no support and needs to rest on trestles or table tops.

A more sophisticated form of frame is freestanding and pivots to an angle that allows a more comfortable working position. Free-standing frames, some of which are beautifully hand-made, can unfortunately prove an expensive outlay for a beginner.

Quilting hoops and small frames

Quilting hoops are sturdy wooden hoops that secure fabric layers between an inner and outer hoop by means of a wooden clamp. Small frames are now made of plastic tube over which the fabric layers are secured with plastic 'grips'. The quilt is moved within the hoop or frame as stitching progresses and tensioned by means of the clamp or grips.

Both freestanding and lap-held hoops and tube frames can be purchased in a variety of sizes. The smaller lap versions, in particular, are light, easy to rotate to a comfortable working position, and

Devices for holding quilt layers together range in size from large frames to small hoops. The forms of freestanding frames and hoops, in which the quilt is held at an angle, can be more comfortable to work at.

portable. They are also relatively inexpensive and are therefore an ideal choice for the beginner.

Hoops and tube frames can, however, crush fabrics and are not recommended for silk. They should always be removed from a quilt when you have finished stitching for the time being.

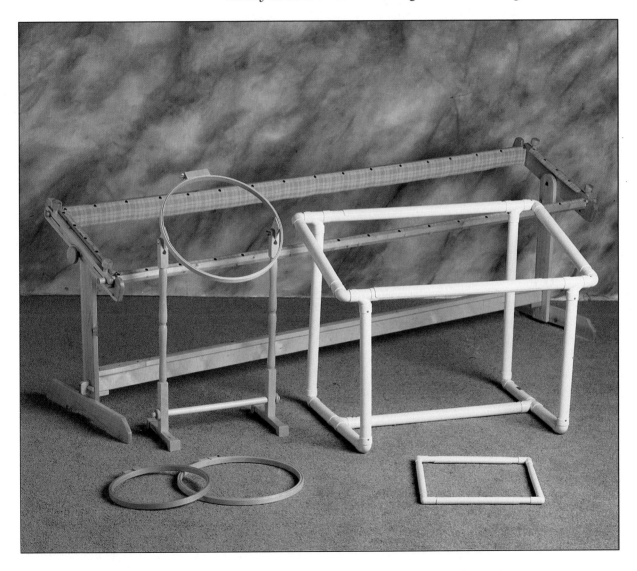

Marking tools

The tool you use to mark your quilting design on the fabric must be chosen very carefully. No single marker can be recommended for all fabrics because of variables of colour, texture and fabric surface. Also consider whether you intend to quilt with a hoop or small tube frame, both of which require the quilt to be handled constantly, and whether you can wash the quilt to remove any lines of marking.

Before starting a quilt, it is advisable to mark and stitch a trial piece with your chosen marker and fabric, to see how clearly the marks show to your eyes, whether the lines show after stitching and whether they can be removed by sponging or washing.

Chalk-based markers Chalk-based markers include dressmakers' chalk pencils, and powdered chalk markers, both of which are available in selected colours.

Chalk markers leave a clear line which often disappears during quilting or is easily erased (by brush or fabric rubber). A chalk pencil must, however, be kept sharp to avoid thick lines. Neither form of chalk marker is particularly suitable if you are quilting in a hoop or tube frame, because the constant handling removes the marks.

Pencils Silver pencils and soapstone pencils are among the most popular markers supplied by specialist shops. Both types will produce clear lines, almost invisible after quilting, on a variety of fabrics. Coloured pencils, of the same colour but a darker tone than that of the fabric, can also be used, leaving barely visible lines when quilted. With water-erasable pencils, the lines are sponged away with cold water after stitching.

White or cream fabrics present particular difficulties. Lead pencils can be used with care if an appropriate kind is chosen. Do not use 'school-type' pencils, but obtain a mechanical or propelling pencil which can be fitted with a 0.5mm ($\frac{1}{50}$in) lead – the finest possible for practical use. An H lead is normally the best choice, though if you have difficulty seeing the hard, fine line you can use an HB. As long as a very light hand is used in drawing, the lines should not show after quilting nor should the graphite work into the thread.

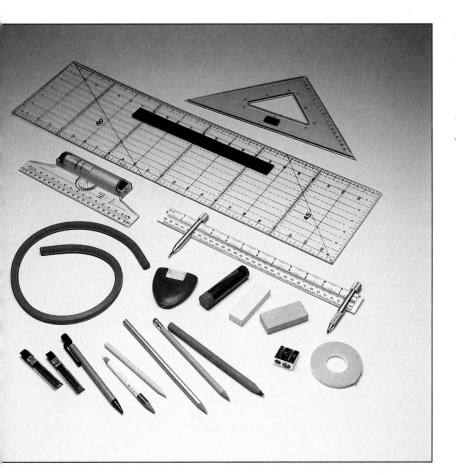

It is vital to choose a suitable fabric marker. Those illustrated here include chalk pencils, a powdered chalk wheel and 'lipstick'-type applicator, a silver pencil, a soapstone pencil, a mechanical pencil, a water erasable pencil, and quilters' tape. The other tools shown are a large quilters' ruler, a rolling ruler, a set square, a flexible curve and a long-rule compass.

Quilters' tape   Re-usable masking tape, if placed lightly on fabric, provides a firm guideline for straight-line patterns.

Other marking equipment

A large ruler is the other essential marking tool, but the quilting market is flooded with a variety of markers for lines, angles and curves. Some are gimmicky and of limited use; others are invaluable. Personal favourites are flexible curves and the quilters' ruler, which is ready marked with dimensions and angles. It is worth browsing around artists' suppliers for other useful tools.

19

Preparing for quilting

A quilt is, basically, a textile sandwich with a fabric cover on the top and bottom and the batting inside. Quilts can be reversible, with both covers intended for use and show, but more usually one side is the decorative quilt top and the reverse is a backing fabric.

Careful preparation is needed to prevent the quilt layers moving and puckering during stitching. The precise method of preparation depends on whether you intend to quilt by hand or machine and, if hand quilting, whether you will use a large frame, a hoop or a tube frame.

Note, however, that the quilting design should always be marked on the quilt top (or top cover) before this preparation stage. The techniques involved are covered in Chapter 4.

LARGE QUILTS

1 Mark the centre and the mid-point of the four edges on all layers. Centre the bottom layer on a large table, wrong side up, securing the surplus with clips.

SMALL QUILTS

1 Lay the unmarked (or backing) fabric, wrong side up, on a hard, flat surface, such as a table or the floor; smooth it carefully, and secure it at the corners with tape.

2 Lay the batting over the bottom fabric, smoothing and securing it with tape, as for the backing fabric.

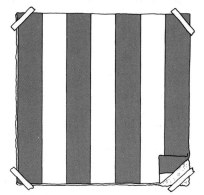

3 Smooth the top over the batting. Tape corners, then pin layers together, from the centre towards the corners and edges. Secure with lines of basting, as described opposite for a large quilt.

2 Fold the batting into quarters. Match the corners of the batting to the centre point and edges of one quarter of the bottom layer, and then open out the batting in place over the bottom layer. Without stretching the batting, smooth it gently outwards.

3 Fold the top into quarters, with the right side in. Matching the centre point and centre edges with those on the batting, open it out, and smooth and pin it in position. Once you have pinned the area on the table surface, smooth the three layers of the outer areas of the quilt in turn, and pin them in position.

4 Secure the layers together with lines of basting stitches 10–15cm (4–6in) apart, both across and down the quilt. Always baste from the centre outwards, beginning with a long length of thread and leaving half of it at the centre, to be rethreaded for the other half of the line. Basting stitches are removed when quilting is completed.

For machine quilting, safety pins can be used in place of basting threads, which tend to catch on the presser foot of the machine.

Layering

When hand quilting is held in a hoop or tube frame, or when you are machine quilting, the fabrics for the quilt sandwich need to be smoothed out, layered together and secured, either with basting stitches or safety pins. (Only use safety pins if you can be sure that they will not leave pin marks in your fabric.)

The fabric layers must first be cut to size – with an allowance on all sides for finishing, and for the small reduction in size that will take place during quilting – and then carefully pressed.

Setting in a large frame

When it is worked in a large frame, a quilt does *not* need to be basted together. Following this time-honoured method of setting, the quilt layers stay firmly tensioned and in position.

 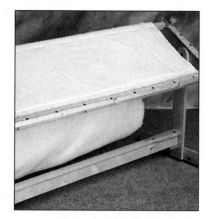 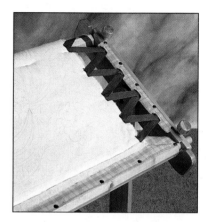

1 Mark the centre point of the webbing on each rail and of the top and bottom fabric edges. Tack the (unmarked) backing fabric, wrong side up, to the webbing fixed to each rail, matching centre points. Roll the fabric on to the far rail until about 45cm (18in) is left, then fix the rails and stretchers in position, with the fabric flat but not too taut.

2 Lay the batting over the bottom layer, edge to edge. Smooth carefully, allowing any surplus to hang over the far rail. Lay the quilt top over the batting, marked side up and edge to edge, and smooth it out. Next, tack the batting and quilt top to the webbing along the near rail. At the far rail, pin through all three layers, using fine pins or size 10 quilting needles. Fold up the quilt top and batting where they hang over the far rail, to prevent them touching the floor.

3 Tension the two side edges of the quilt with a 2.5cm (1in) wide tape, looped over the stretchers or pinned to the side webbing, then pinned in position through the quilt layers. Leave some flexibility in the tensioned layers for ease of stitching – enough to take several running stitches at a time.

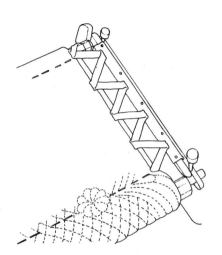

SETTING IN A HOOP

A TUBE FRAME

4 Quilt progressively across the top to the far rail. Remove pins and tapes; loosen the rails and stretchers to roll the completed section on to the near rail, and unroll a new part of the bottom layer. Smooth the batting and quilt top over this as before, then re-pin and re-tape, ready to quilt. Repeat until quilting is completed.

Smooth out the layered quilt and place the inner ring of the hoop under the area that you intend to work. Unscrew the clamp, and lay the outer hoop over the quilt so that it fits over the inner hoop. Ensure that the layers are evenly stretched in the hoop and are not puckered, at either the front or back. Tighten the clamp, but leave enough flexibility to allow several running stitches to be taken with ease. Work from the centre outwards in a radial fashion.

To set the assembled layers in a tube frame, smooth them out, and then lay the tube part of the frame under the quilt. Secure the quilt to the frame by fixing the 'grips' over the quilt on all four sides of the frame. Adjust to a flexible tension by sliding the grips on the frame.

Finishing techniques

When quilting is finally completed, and the quilt has been removed from its hoop or frame, the edges need to be finished. An ill-considered or inappropriately finished edge can spoil the visual impact of a quilt, so think about how you will finish the edges as you plan your quilt, not while it is in the making.

FOLDED EDGES

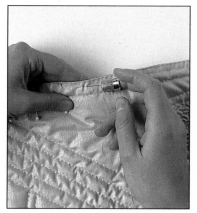

Trim the cover fabrics to within 2.5cm (1in) and the batting to within 6mm (¼in) of the outer quilted line around the quilt edge. Fold in the raw edges of the covers to within 1.2cm (½in) of the outer quilted line; align them together, and pin in position. Stitch along the edge with either a double or single row of machine or hand-sewn stitches.

BINDING STRIP

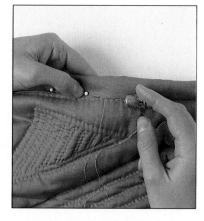

Use either one of the fabrics in the quilt or a contrast fabric; bias strips are not required unless the outer edges are curved or the corners are very rounded. The binding strip should be cut twice the desired finished width of the edging, plus 1.2cm (½in), for two seam allowances. Turn in a seam allowance on one short edge of the binding, and trim the three quilt layers – batting and two covers – to a minimum of 1.2cm (½in) from the outer quilted line.

Matching raw edges and with right sides together, pin the binding strip to the quilt, starting in the middle of one side edge. Overlap the folded binding edge with the other raw, short edge, by about 1.2cm (½in). Machine the binding in position, then fold it to the back of the quilt; turn in the raw edge and oversew in position.

SELF BINDING

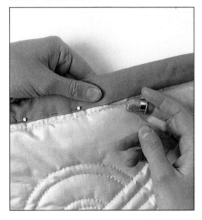

PIPING

SELF PIPING

This can only be done if sufficient allowance – twice the finished width plus one seam allowance – has been left on the back cover. Trim the quilt top *only* to a minimum of 1.2cm (½in) from the outer quilted line. Trim the batting to the required width of the finished binding. Fold the edge of the backing fabric; bring forward, and pin in position, making sure that the batting is at the edge of the quilt. Prepare opposite edges first, then the other two, mitring or making straight folds at the corners. Secure the turnings with oversewn or running stitches, or machine along the folded edge.

Cover piping cord of your chosen thickness with a bias strip of fabric and machine stitch the strip to enclose the cord. Use your zipper foot to stitch close to the cord. Now finish as for folded edges, but insert the covered piping cord between the edges of the cover before stitching them together.

Like self binding, this can only be done if a sufficient allowance – 2cm (¾in) plus enough fabric to enclose the piping cord – has been left on one cover. Trim the other cover to within 2cm (¾in) of the outer quilted line and pin it back. Trim the batting to within 1.2cm (½in) of the outer quilted line. Lay the piping cord along the trimmed edges of batting. Fold the covering fabric over the cord; pin then tack in position, close to the cord. Unpin the edge of the other cover; turn in the 6mm (¼in) seam allowance and pin the folded edge close to the cord. Tack it in position, then stitch along the folded edge by hand or machine.

CHAPTER 2

HAND AND MACHINE QUILTING

Hand quilting

Hand quilting is still the preferred option for many quilters, and to understand why such a time-intensive method remains so popular, we need to consider the differences between the nature of hand-sewn quilting stitches and a machine-sewn straight stitch. Because it interlocks two threads, the machine produces a flat, continuous line stitch.

A hand-sewn running stitch, on the other hand, produces a line of quite different appearance. The quilted line appears as a series of sunken stitches and raised spaces in which the filling lofts up between the stitches. It is this broken, almost puckered line, with its contrasts of light and depth, which gives hand quilting its particular character and a subtlety of line that cannot be reproduced by machine.

Basic skills
The basic techniques of hand quilting are very simple. The aim is to produce even, straight stitches, and the way to do this is to practise until you develop a relaxed, steady rhythm. Thimbles and finger protectors may feel clumsy at first, but it is worth persevering with them. You will find that it also helps to keep several needles in play at the same time, so that you maintain the flow of continuous lines across the work.

The number of stitches taken to a given measurement will vary with the individual and with the thickness of the batting. If this is very thick, it will be impossible to take as many stitches as it would with a very fine batting. What is more important is that the stitches should be of much the same length and evenly spaced throughout.

Quilt designs from Allendale and Weardale, two of the most northerly English dales, reached their peak in the late 19th and early 20th centuries. Working in the same style, Lilian Hedley has designed an elegant sateen wholecloth quilt, Echoes of the Past. *Size: 224cm × 224cm (90in × 90in).*

STARTING A THREAD

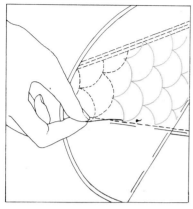

Take a thread about 45cm (18in) long, preferably waxed, with a single knot at the end. Push the needle into the quilt top, about 2cm (¾in) from the line that you intend to quilt, and bring the needle up on the line, without going through the back cover. Pull the thread through until the knot is at the quilt top, then gently pull it through the fabric to bury it in the filling.

THE RUNNING STITCH

Push the needle tip through the quilt layers until, with the hand below the work, you can draw the needle out through the bottom layer, then guide it back up to the top. Pull the thread through firmly, to make two stitches – one above and one below. With practice, you will be able to take several stitches together by using the thimble on the middle finger of your (top) quilting hand to rock the needle up and down before pulling the thread through. Use the thumb of your quilting hand to press down the fabric ahead of the stitches.

MOVING

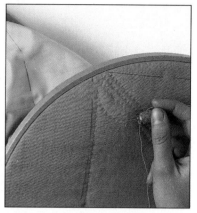

If you have reached the end of a pattern line but still have sufficient thread to continue, move the needle through the filling to another pattern line. In practice, this can only be done if the line is less than a needle-length away.

TRAVELLING

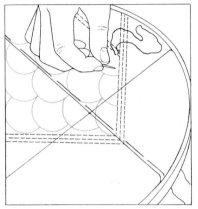

FINISHING

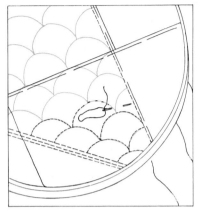

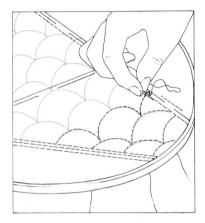

If you need to cover a wider gap, travel the needle through the quilt to the next quilting line. To do this, push the needle through the filling as far as possible in the direction of the new line and through to the quilt top. Pull the needle part way through, then swivel it around and push it, eye first, in the required direction. Push the needle eye part way up through the top, swivel, and repeat the process until you have reached the required pattern line.

1 When finishing a thread part way along a line, make a back stitch, then run the thread through the filling, taking a few tiny stitches, about 2cm (¾in) apart, along the unstitched line. Run the thread through the filling again, then cut it off. The tiny stitches will be anchored by succeeding stitches along the line.

2 At the end of a pattern line, backstitch, bringing the needle up through the hole at the end of the stitch, leaving a small loop. Push the needle through the loop, taking it back down the same hole and through, to anchor in the filling. Run the thread as far as possible through the filling before coming up. Cut the end on the quilt surface.

QUILTING CURVES

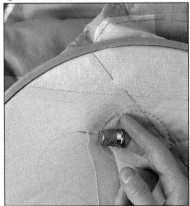

When quilting curved lines, it may be necessary to take only one stitch at a time if the curve is a tight one. When a curved line is part of both the outline and the inner detail of a pattern – for example, the petal outlines of a rose pattern – quilt it as one line to prevent an angular join where the outer and inner lines meet.

Machine quilting

It goes without saying that quilting by machine is quicker than hand stitching, but it must be stressed that it is essentially different to hand quilting. Whatever stitches and threads are used, the machined line is continuous and flat, in contrast to the broken, lofted line of hand quilting. Because this continuous line depresses the filling more, there is less loft between the stitched lines of machine quilting and none at all between the stitches. If that sounds a bit technical, think of it this way – there are no 'bumps' along a machine-stitched line, only stitches.

It is important to understand this visual difference and to work *with* the character of machine quilting. If you try to use the machine to duplicate the qualities of hand-stitched pieces, you will be disappointed.

Machine quilting does not have to be confined to a straight line stitch, especially if you have an automatic, electronic or state-of-the-art computerized machine. These machines are versatile tools, capable of a wide range of stitches, all of which can be varied in length and width. Free machining offers even greater scope for creativity, so get to know the capabilities of your own machine and experiment with it. Always keep your machine in good working order, and make sure that it is correctly set up and tensioned before you begin to quilt.

Speed and versatility are the machine's great assets, but there are some technical difficulties, especially in the case of large quilts, that need to be considered. The fabric layers will almost certainly move and pucker unless they have been very carefully assembled and held together. It is also necessary to have a suitable mechanism or attachment to feed the layers through evenly. Because the machine works at a much faster pace than the hand, the pattern lines need to be bolder and easier for the eye to pick up, so it is vital to choose a suitable marker. Manipulating a large quilt through the machine can be tricky, but this problem can be overcome either by following established techniques or with the 'quilt-as-you-go' method.

If you are quilting by machine, it helps to choose continuous line patterns, so that stopping and restarting the machine is kept to a minimum.

This masterly pillow, drawn and painted by hand, is part of the counterpane and pillow set Creation, *commissioned from Paddy Killer for the crafts house in the Gateshead Garden Festival. Made in silk, cotton, velvet and hand-printed cotton, the embroidery includes machine quilting with cotton and rayon thread. Size: 75cm × 75cm (30in × 30in). (Photograph courtesy of the Tyne and Wear Museum Service.)*

Automatic machining

With automatic machining, the feed dogs that feed the fabric through the machine are up and functioning. Feed dogs, however, only work on the lowest layer of fabric and, with the three layers of a batted quilt, this results in some differential in the movement of the layers. A means of pushing the top and bottom layers together must be found. This can be achieved in two ways – either by using a machine equipped with a dual feed mechanism, or by fitting an attachment known as a walking foot.

SETTING UP

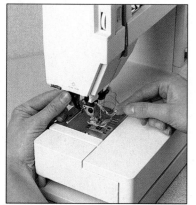

Set your machine for dual feed or fit a walking foot. Choose your stitch and set the machine accordingly; check the tension. For straight stitching, choose a stitch length of approximately eight stitches to every 2.5cm (1in). For grid quilting, fit a quilting bar.

STARTING AND STOPPING

1 For straight stitch, bring both threads to the top surface, to prevent snarling of the bobbin thread, by taking a single stitch manually. Begin forward stitching with the stitch length set at zero and gradually increase over the first 1cm (⅜in) to the required length. To finish a line of stitching, reduce the stitch length over the last 1cm (⅜in) down to zero at the end of the line. Snip threads above and below.

2 For decorative stitches, again bring both threads to the top surface. Begin and end with a forward stitch, leaving about 15cm (6in) of thread at the top and bottom; the threads can be secured with a needle on the reverse of the quilt when machining is completed.

This completed sample was first quilted with straight-line quilting, using a quilting bar as the line guide. After this, torn strips were overlaid and stitched, using an automatic decorative stitch and shiny rayon thread.

TURNING ANGLES

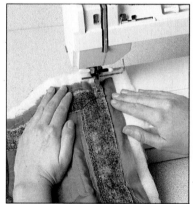

Slow the speed of stitching as you come close to the angled turn and stop, with the needle down, at the apex. Lift the presser foot and reposition the quilt, ensuring that no sections are dragging against the needle. Continue forward stitching.

Automatic machining with a straight stitch is suitable for 'quilt-in-the-ditch' patterns, for patterns formed by straight lines and sharp angles, or even for large-scale curved patterns. It is much more difficult, however, to use automatic stitching to quilt curved patterns that require constant movement and changes of direction.

In addition to quilting with a straight stitch, bear in mind that decorative machine stitches can create a variety of textures and original effects on your work.

33

Free machining

With free machining, the fabric layers are not fed automatically through the machine but are moved by hand. This allows the fabric to move in any direction and at any speed. Free machining is the best way to straight stitch small-scale curvilinear patterns or meander lines, though zigzag stitching can also be worked with this technique.

Successful free machining is an acquired skill. You will require some practice before you are able to follow a line and at the same time maintain an even stitch length, using just your hands to work the fabric through the machine, but it is worth persevering with the techniques. Once mastered, free machining opens up a whole world of decorative machine stitching – as well as enabling you to quilt around curves!

In order to prevent the fabric from being fed through automatically, it is necessary to disengage the feed dogs. The feed dogs can be lowered on most machines, but in some cases there is a plate attachment that can be used to cover the feed dogs so that they do not touch the fabric.

SETTING UP

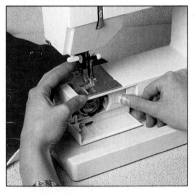

Lower or cover the feed dogs; disengage any dual feed mechanism, and fit a darning foot. Check the tension, then set the stitch length to zero to prevent any movement of the feed dogs snagging the lowest layer.

STITCHING

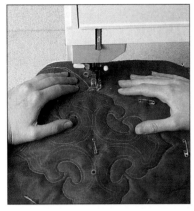

Bring both threads to the top surface. Take several tiny stitches by moving the fabric gently to and fro, to lock the threads. With fingers slightly extended and hands either side of the needle, stitch along the pattern lines, controlling the stitch length by the speed with which you push the fabric. Maintain a steady, fairly high running speed and do not rotate the fabric. Finish with several tiny stitches and trim loose threads.

The oriental feel of Barbara Howell's Hashad quilt has been created by assembling pieced blocks of multicoloured cotton and polycotton fabrics. These were quilted with automatic and free machine stitches onto a thin polyester batting and a cotton backing. Size: 122cm × 198cm (48in × 78in).

Quilt-as-you-go

The technique known as quilt-as-you-go is an ideal way to overcome the problem of manipulating a large quilt around the machine. The quilt is broken down into smaller sections of any size or shape; these are quilted individually before being joined together in order to finish the quilt.

Quilt-as-you-go is also a popular technique for hand quilting in a hoop or small frame, especially if the work is to be portable, or if the

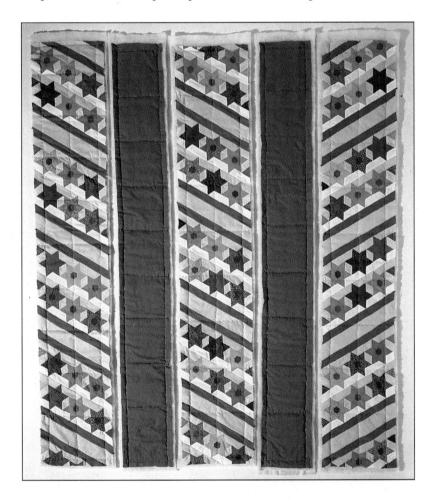

Anne Tuck has separately layered each strip to prepare Three Heads are Better than One *for quilting. On the pieced strips, she will quilt-in-the-ditch, so no marking is necessary, but on the other strips she has marked the quilting design, which links the changing directions of the stars pattern. Size: 168cm × 203cm (66in × 80in).*

1 Layer each unit of the quilt in the usual way, having first marked out the quilting design. Allow *at least* 1cm (⅜in) on each side of the unit for seams. Quilt units separately, by hand or machine, keeping the quilting free of the seam allowances.

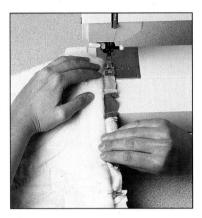 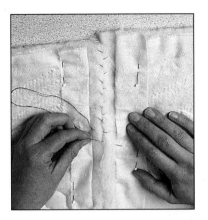 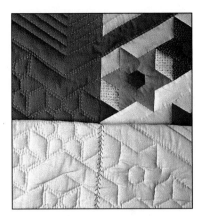

2 Lay the units out on a flat surface in their correct position. Work out a sequence for joining the units: for example, join blocks into rows before completion. Take adjoining units, fold back the batting and bottom layer and, with right sides together, seam the quilt top only. Neaten and press seams.

3 Open out the quilt and trim away surplus batting until the batting edges butt against each other. Stitch these together, using a ladder or herringbone stitch. Use a light-coloured thread, though in the quilt illustrated a dark thread has been used for clarity.

4 Finally, fold one edge of the unattached bottom layer over the unfolded edge of the adjacent unit and hand sew into position, using either a blind stitch or decorative feather stitch. Add borders and edge the quilt as required.

bulk and weight of a large quilt would prove a problem during stitching.

A variety of quilt types – traditional quilts of square or rectangular blocks, strip quilts – can be quilted in this way, especially if the quilt is composed of units within which the patterns are contained. Unless you have had a lot of experience, it is not easy to match up quilting lines from one unit to the next, especially if they are closely spaced. For this reason, finely worked wholecloth quilts cannot be successfully quilted in this way.

Machining large quilts

If quilt-as-you-go is not a realistic option for a large quilt, then it is possible to machine stitch even a quilt of double-bed size, using the techniques developed in America by Harriet Hargrave. Two problems need to be overcome: the weight of the quilt will tend to drag it away from the needle during stitching, and its bulk may prove difficult to feed through the machine.

After careful layering, place the quilt on a flat surface and fold the area to the *left* of the first section to be stitched into folds of about 25cm (10in). The area to the *right* of the section to be stitched is tightly rolled. Use bicycle clips to hold this roll in position, if necessary. These folds and roll should enable you to feed the quilt through the machine, though you will find it necessary to continually refold and reroll as you work across the quilt. Set up your machine on a large table, arranging it so that the table top will take the weight of the quilt once it has been fed through the machine. The bulk of the quilt that is still to be fed through should either be kept on your lap or even laid over your shoulder, so that it can be fed *downwards* to the needle. This should prevent the problem of dragging.

The sequence of stitching will depend on the design that you have chosen. If you are machine quilting in a grid, quilt the centre line first from top to bottom, then work outwards to the right. Turn the quilt end to end and quilt the other side from the centre outwards. For other designs, it is also advisable, as a general rule, to start at the centre and work outwards.

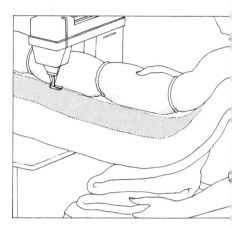

1 In order to feed the full quilt through the machine, the left-hand section needs to be folded, and the right-hand section tightly rolled and secured with cycle clips. As quilting progresses, you will need to re-fold and re-roll the quilt.

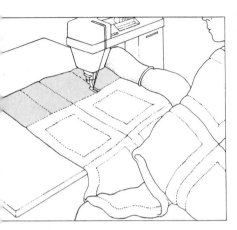

2 The folded and rolled quilt is fed downwards onto the machine, to prevent drag. Set your machine on a table top with space to the back and left side of the machine, to take the weight of the quilt.

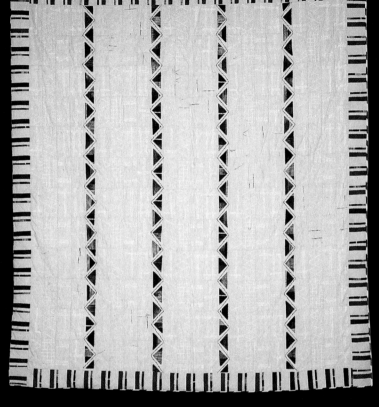

Inspired by African textiles, Carole Kokinis machine-couched silk, cotton and mixed blend threads to calico blocks then pieced these with coloured strips to form the Calico Quilt. *The fully-pieced quilt was machine quilted 'in-the-ditch' around the blocks, and a surface wave pattern machined on the border. Size: 249cm × 264cm (98in × 104in). (Photograph courtesy of the Tyne and Wear Museum Service.)*

Quilting through paper

Some delicate fabrics, such as silk, are difficult to mark for machine quilting. For small quilts, quilt-as-you-go sections or garment pieces, it is possible to mark your design on tracing paper. Attach this to the fabric top, and quilt through the paper, following the drawn lines. The paper is then removed after quilting.

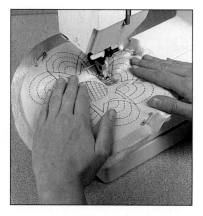

1 Draw the design boldly on tracing paper. Curves are easier to draw with broken lines rather than continuous ones, and show up just as well. Baste the pattern to the layered quilt or quilt section, or attach it with safety pins.

2 Using the techniques already described for stopping and starting, stitch through the paper and quilt layers, following the pattern. This method is suitable for either automatic or free machining.

3 When stitching is completed, pull away the tracing paper. For closely quilted areas, use the blunt end of a seam ripper to remove all traces of paper.

The intricate design on My Marcella Quilt *was adapted by Peggie Stenner from her grandmother's white Marcella quilt. Such manufactured quilts were highly fashionable bed covers around 1900. Size: 120cm × 230cm (48in × 91in).*

CHAPTER 3

PATTERNS FOR QUILTING

Patterns in quilting are the basic units that make up a design; the way in which these patterns are combined is the key to quilting design. If you think of quilting patterns as line drawings, then the quilting lines represent pen or pencil lines.

In theory, whatever you can draw you can quilt, but it is not so easy in practice. Quilting lines, when stitched, are *not* part of a flat, two-dimensional area. They are the receding lines of a three-dimensional, softly sculptured surface, and not all forms of line decoration or illustration translate easily into textile relief. For quilting, most patterns need strongly defined lines, and it is important to consider the relationship between the areas where the batting rises up between the lines of stitching (positive areas) and those where it is depressed (negative areas).

Quilting patterns can be broadly grouped into motifs, border patterns and filling patterns, according to the part they play in the design as a whole. The different elements of an overall pattern, or the pattern as a whole, will tend to fall into one of the categories below.

Naturalistic designs represent forms found in nature, such as leaves, flowers and animals.
Geometric patterns are based on shapes, such as circles, squares or triangles.
Representational (graphic) designs feature images representing people, places or objects.
Symbolic images, such as hearts (love) or pineapples (hospitality), occur in many designs.

Patterns may also belong to particular decorative styles. Celtic and *art nouveau* patterns represent two historically distant styles, and many traditional quilting patterns bear a close resemblance to other forms of folk art.

Assembled in blocks of cotton and cotton lawn, using the quilt-as-you-go technique, Doreen Hallett's Checkerboard *represents a sampler quilt of traditional quilting patterns. Because the quilt was made as a gift, its size and shape were carefully designed for a particular bed. Size: 193cm × 218cm (76in × 86in).*

Motif patterns

Motifs can be used singly, or as symmetrical repeats, or in organized groups. They are complete patterns, with outlines that do not need to interlock with other pattern units, and the manner in which they are used within a design makes a vital contribution to the strength (or weakness) of that design. An isolated motif stitched here or there on the surface of a quilt usually does little to enhance the overall design, whereas a composite pattern of repeated motifs can be a strong focal point within the whole image.

A wide range of naturalistic, symbolic and geometric motifs is an important element in the library of traditional patterns. Certain motifs, and the way in which they are used, have become character-istic of particular regions or cultures with a long tradition of quilting. For example, spiral motifs are associated with Welsh quilts, quilted basket patterns with Amish quilts from America and feather patterns with the quilts made in Northern England. Besides traditional patterns, an infinite variety of representational and abstract motifs can be developed.

Motifs should be *positive* elements of the quilt surface, clearly standing up in relief. For hand quilting, particularly, motifs need a strong sense of line definition, otherwise the broken nature of the hand-stitched line blurs the image. For this reason, complex 'picture' patterns seldom work well on hand-quilted pieces.

Most motif patterns are drawn with templates, though some can be drawn freehand. Avoid being too restrictive in your choice of motifs – especially if you are decorating a wholecloth quilt. The most successful quilting designs of this type are usually those that combine a variety of motifs. In this context, it is worth considering making your own templates rather than relying on purchased ones, for you will then have a much wider choice of patterns.

TRADITIONAL MOTIFS

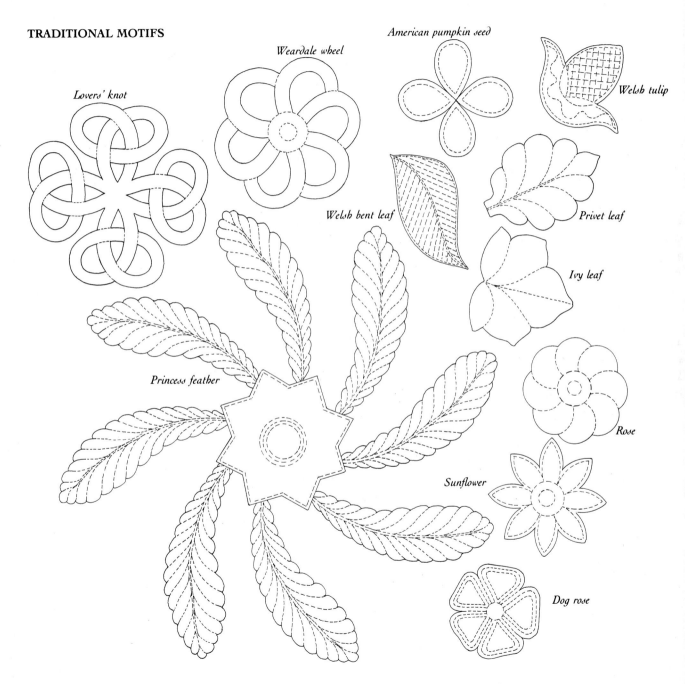

Lovers' knot

Weardale wheel

American pumpkin seed

Welsh tulip

Welsh bent leaf

Privet leaf

Ivy leaf

Princess feather

Rose

Sunflower

Dog rose

CELTIC AND FOLK ART MOTIFS

REPRESENTATIONAL MOTIFS

Border patterns

On traditional quilts, border patterns either frame the central area of a quilt or are worked down the panels, in the case of a strip quilt. But there is no reason why their usefulness should be limited, and they can fill any long, narrow area on a quilt surface.

Border patterns are generally built up in one of three ways: by repeating motifs; by using interlocking patterns; or by dividing the strip into geometric divisions. Whichever type of pattern is used, it is essential to ensure that it fits correctly into the border length.

The importance of borders on traditional-style quilts is often overlooked, but they are an essential element in holding together a design and, on pieced or appliquéd quilts, they may be the most readily identifiable element of the quilting design. Even on contemporary quilts, the use of border patterns still, in many cases, remains conservative, so you will have a wide freedom of choice, with scope either to develop new pattern ideas or to rework old ones.

The simple pieced cotton shapes on Emily Brown's Springtime *are complemented by her considered choice of quilting patterns within the design areas of this medallion-style quilt. Size: 206cm × 224cm (81in × 90in).*

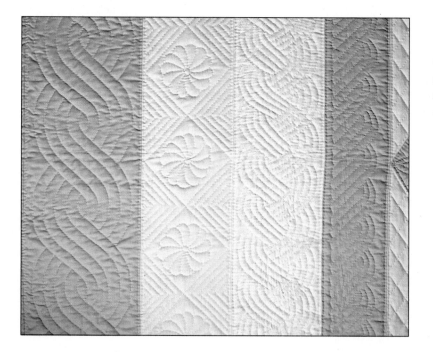

The four border patterns of Springtime *include the ever-popular cable twist and plait patterns, together with a simple geometric border and a contemporary pattern idea.*

TRADITIONAL BORDER PATTERNS

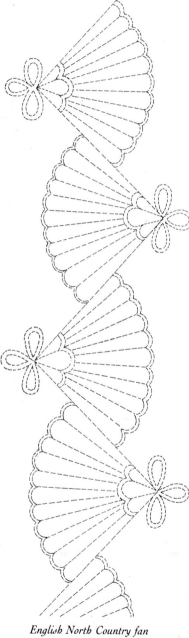

English North Country fan

Welsh geometric

American-style feather

Celtic knot pattern   *Two border patterns from folk art sources*

Borders and corners

When border patterns are used around the four sides of a quilt, framing the central area of the design, some thought must be given to the corners, where the border strips meet. In practice, there are three ways of dealing with corners of borders, the first being to turn the pattern around the corner in such a way that the continuity is maintained and the complete border then appears as a whole, with all four sides unbroken.

The second is to stop the border pattern at the corner and insert a square between the two adjacent sides of the pattern. The square can be filled with any chosen pattern – on traditional quilts, a motif or simple filling pattern was usually worked. The pattern then appears on the completed quilt as four border lengths with squares between.

A third solution to the problem is to continue the two adjacent sides of the border pattern until they are very close together, then link them with a sympathetic pattern – a simple freehand one is a

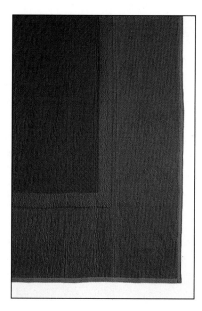

The classic Amish method of working a feather pattern around a corner is illustrated in the detail of this quilt, Square Within a Square, *made in Pennsylvania around 1895. (Photograph by Sharon Risedorph and Lynn Kellner, courtesy of the Esprit Quilt Collection, San Francisco.)*

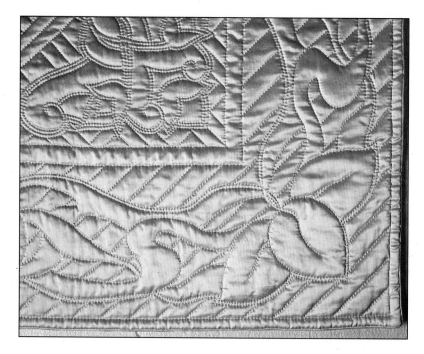

On For Michelle, *Brenda Johnstone incorporated a corner motif into her border pattern, in this way maintaining the flow and character of the design.*

possibility. In this case, the finished border pattern is 'interrupted' at the corners but, if the link has been carefully thought out, the design is not weakened.

Traditionally, all three possibilities have been worked on quilts, with a heavy preference for the second – the simplest! Designing a continuous pattern around a corner was a problem avoided by all but the most skilful of pattern makers.

Your choice of corner treatment will depend as much on the design of the top to be quilted as on your drafting skills. If you are quilting a pieced border for a pattern which is itself broken by pieced corner squares, then the second option may well be the most appropriate. On a wholecloth quilt, however, such a solution may inadequately frame the central design; continuing the pattern around the corner will give a more complete look to the design. It is possible to obtain templates of linking patterns to turn corners, the disadvantage being that if you rely on these, your choice of borders will be restricted to those for which you can buy templates.

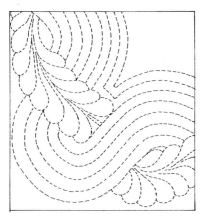

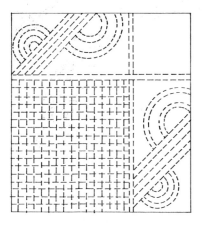

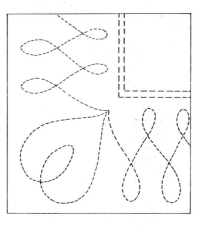

1 The English 'North Country' feather twist pattern is turned at the corner to maintain its continuity.

2 This geometric pattern is broken at the corner by a square, with a simple filling pattern inside.

3 This curvilinear pattern is linked at the corner with a heart motif.

Filling patterns

These patterns fill the spaces between motif and border patterns on the quilt surface. Their purpose is to fill space and to focus attention on the other elements of the design. For this reason, filling patterns can be considered the negative areas of the design and should recede visually from the positive motif and border patterns. To achieve this, they are usually worked with closer lines of stitching.

Motif and border patterns themselves often contain areas of filling within the patterns. These, too, should be closely quilted if they are to create an effective contrast with the more lofted areas of the patterns.

A filling pattern can also be used, on its own, over the entire surface of a quilt. In this case, its purpose is to provide simple decoration and hold the layers in place without conflicting visually with a pieced or appliquéd design on the quilt.

On Green Maze, *Inger Milburn has used a simple hand-stitched filling pattern to give a textured quality to the white cotton background of the quilt. A single flower motif (left) is used as a central focus to the quilting design. Size: 132cm × 132cm (52in × 52in).*

SQUARE DIAMONDS

SHELL

WAVE

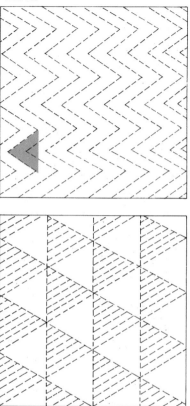

This, the most commonly used and most ancient filling pattern, consists of diagonal lines crossing at right angles (top). The basic pattern can be simply varied by a double set of lines, known as double lining (above), or triple lining if three rows are used.

Although it is simple in plan, and requires no template to mark it out, you will need to take great care when drawing this pattern on a quilt top, in order to keep the angles of intersection correct.

Based on a semicircular outline, this pattern (top) is best drawn either with a semicircular template or a full shell-shaped template.

Any size of shell-shape can be used, and the pattern may be varied by double or triple lining, and by filling the shell shapes with motifs or other filling patterns (above).

Popular on early 19th-century quilts, and on Irish quilts, this simple chevron pattern is drawn with a template based on an equal-sided triangle. The template is placed in rows running down or across the quilt, and the basic pattern drawn around the sides of the template, any intervening chevron lines being drawn with a ruler (top).

The shape can be varied according to how the triangles are connected or filled in (above).

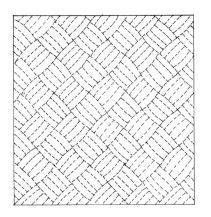

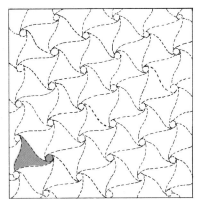

Celtic patterns of all kinds can be adapted for quilting, and celtic key or labyrinth patterns make particularly good filling patterns. This one is based on a diamond grid.

Weave patterns are usually based on a square grid. They can be drawn either with straight lines or, as here, with sinuously-woven outlines, giving a more fluid pattern.

This pattern of curving triangles uses two templates for its construction – a small circle, and a curved triangle shape which is rotated around it.

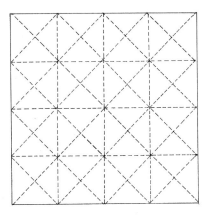

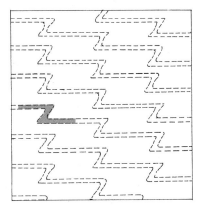

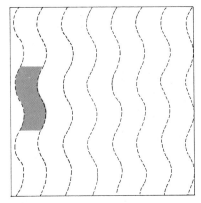

Simple grid patterns can be used either in place of, or together with, the more traditional square diamonds (or hanging squares) infill. Drawn only with a ruler, care is needed to maintain accurate angles and directions.

The sharply-angular nature of a zigzag pattern can be softened by curving the inside angles of the bends in the pattern. Such patterns can be drawn with a template in the form of a single elongated 'Z'.

Though wavy-line patterns are most often used as border patterns in quilting, they make simple and effective filling patterns too. To maintain a consistent length and width of curve, they should be drawn with a template.

Ideas for new patterns

Creating your own patterns is stimulating and fun. To design something unique is deeply satisfying, but all too often the cry 'I am not very good with ideas' is heard from students who are being encouraged to develop their own patterns.

Most new ideas come from using your eyes. Pattern is everywhere, so much so that many decorated everyday objects never receive a second glance. Have you ever studied the patterns on a bank note or inside an envelope, for example?

Because quilting is chiefly a form of line decoration, ideas for patterns can come from all kinds of objects – past and present, large and small – on which line decoration forms a significant part of the surface ornamentation. On a domestic scale, fabrics, wallpapers, tiles, ceramics and glassware are decorated everyday objects; on a larger scale, architectural forms of all kinds – ironwork, stonework, brickwork, windows and doors – can provide ideas for pattern decoration. Church architecture and all forms of folk art are particularly rich sources of ideas. Do not hesitate to develop pattern ideas drawn from such sources – everyone absorbs and abstracts designs from elsewhere, adapting them as necessary. And do not rely on fickle memory; keep a file of sketches and other illustrations, taken as and when you see objects with pattern potential.

Rita Humphry is inspired by church architecture, and her quilts are pieced in individual style, using silk fabrics. This stunning piece, Hereford *(photograph by Richard Hookway), includes cord quilting within the central pattern and elegant curved borders quilted with an arched design. Size: 98cm × 98cm (39in × 39in).*

Pattern decoration on buildings like this French tiled floor (top left), Norwegian folk painting from the early nineteenth century (bottom left), carved oak house support in Kent (below middle) and arched window in Sissinghurst (below), can be easily translated into quilting patterns. (Photographs by IMP/William Mason/Marie-Louise Avery.)

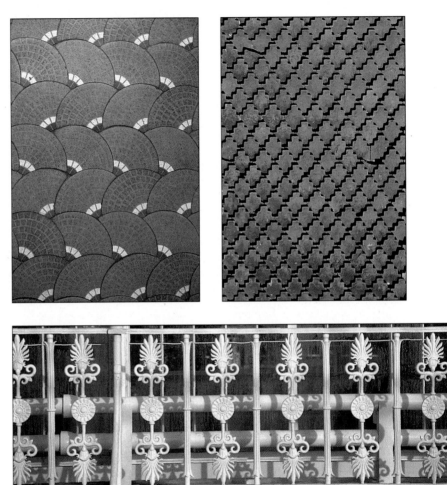

Decorative wall tiles, like those in Macau (above), the wall mosaic in Burgundy (above right) and Victorian office tiles in South East England (far right), can inspire pattern ideas; decorative wrought ironwork, such as these railings in South West London (right), also provides pattern possibilities. (Photographs by IMP/William Mason/Marie-Louise Avery.)

Templates

For some motifs, border and filling patterns you will require templates, especially if the patterns are to be repeated in a design. The templates are used either as an aid to drawing patterns directly on the quilt surface or when drafting a full-scale design on paper. (Reduced-scale templates are also a useful tool when you wish to map out a design on a small scale during the planning stages.)

Templates should be of stiff paper, cardboard or plastic. You can buy them ready for use, but many are simple to make. Template plastic, or mylar, from specialist suppliers is easy to cut with scissors, and the ability to make your own templates will give you greater flexibility of size and pattern.

Outline templates

With these, only the pattern outlines can be drawn; internal details will need to be filled in by hand. This is not the disadvantage it may seem. If you use an outline template, you are free to fill the shape in a variety of ways, according to choice, and the need to draw internal lines both encourages and sharpens your drawing skills.

Outline templates can be home-made, though useful sheets of paper outlines of many traditional patterns are commercially available; for practical purposes, these should be cut out and mounted on cardboard or plastic.

Stencil templates

Plastic stencil templates have the internal pattern lines cut away in the form of long dashes, so they act as guides for both external and internal lines. This is quick, convenient and produces identically-detailed repeats. The danger, though, is that this perfection tends to result in patterns that are mechanical and lifeless elements within a design as a whole, lacking the rhythmic quality that may come from hand-drawn work.

Stencil templates can be made at home: all you will require is card or template plastic and suitable equipment for cutting internal lines. Popular traditional patterns can also be bought in stencil form from specialist suppliers.

These pattern outlines are skilfully produced on tracing paper, but not all commercially-available patterns are of this quality. If you are buying patterns, look closely at the way in which lines have been drawn.

Popular and widely available from specialist suppliers, stencil templates of traditional and other simple stylized patterns are easy to use.

MAKING TEMPLATES

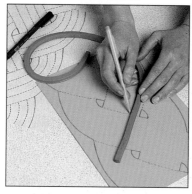

The planned asymmetry of Celtic I by Linda Maltman has been developed from a single filling pattern and celtic knot border patterns. This wholecloth quilt in grey cotton is designed as a panel decoration for a door. Size: 76cm × 198cm (36in × 78in).

1 Draw the pattern, in detail, on matt board or tracing paper. If you are making templates from bought patterns, cut roughly around the shapes, leaving a margin of paper.

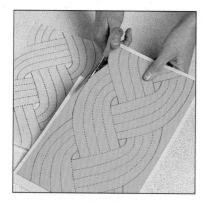

2 Glue the pattern to cardboard or template plastic and cut around it to produce an outline template. Use scissors (curved ones for tight corners and curves), or a cutting mat and craft knife or rotary cutter.

3 To make the outline into a stencil template, cut dashed lines along the internal lines of the pattern, using a craft knife and cutting mat.

CIRCULAR TEMPLATES

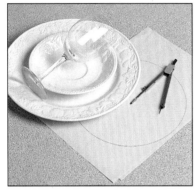

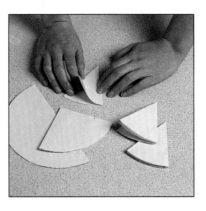

1 Use thin paper – typing paper or greaseproof paper is ideal. Draw a circle to your chosen size using compasses or any suitable circular object – a plate, saucer or glass, for example. Cut out the circle.

2 To create symmetrically shaped edges, fold the circle three times, producing a wedge-shaped segment. Three folds will produce a pattern with an eight-fold symmetry, such as an eight-pointed star; for a 16-edged pattern, fold once more.

3 At the curved edge of the segment, draw cutting lines according to the pattern required: a single scallop for a rose; an inverted 'V' for a star, or a pointed arch for a daisy, sunflower or composite heart. Cut the folded paper along the drawn line. These paper patterns can be made into outline or stencil templates as previously described.

PATTERNS FROM CIRCULAR TEMPLATES

Variety with simple shapes

It is worth acquiring a set of outline templates of simple shapes, each in a range of sizes. These can be used for a variety of different patterns and will be among the most useful templates in any quilter's collection. If you are making your own set of templates, use template plastic for durability – cardboard templates wear out too quickly.

With a little imagination, shapes such as circles, squares and hearts, together with stylized flower templates – roses or tulips, for example – can be used either in whole or in part to create a host of patterns, the variations depending on the different ways in which the shapes are combined and filled in. Many other outline templates have a similar flexibility in the ways that they may be used.

CIRCLE

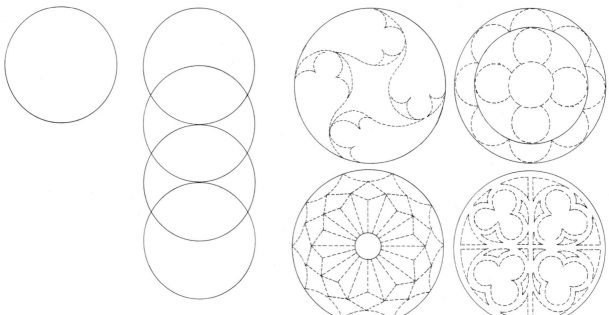

SQUARE

HEART

Patterns without templates

You can draw some patterns without templates by using simple drawing tools, such as a ruler, a set square and compasses. Among the traditional patterns drawn in this way are the types of geometric pattern that were developed by quilters in Wales in the 19th and early 20th centuries. These rely on dividing the pattern areas into simple geometric spaces which are then filled with motifs and filler patterns.

If you follow standard sequences of measuring and marking, geometric patterns of this kind are easily drawn. Despite their basic simplicity, they can be highly decorative when a rich variety of motifs and filling patterns has been used within the geometric spaces.

Patterns without templates can be drawn straight on the fabric, though the beginner would be advised to draw the full-scale design on paper first, before transferring it to fabric.

Right: Borders can be divided into squares, triangles, circles, semicircles and other geometric shapes. Measure the border length, divide evenly, then use ruler or compasses to create the basic divisions: these are then filled with motif and filling patterns.

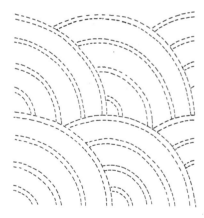
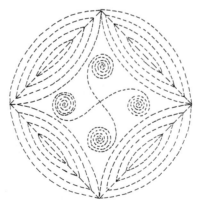
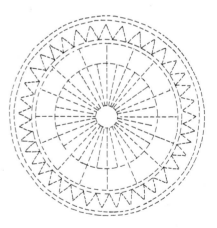

Based on traditional Welsh patterns, these circular and filling patterns are drawn with a ruler and compasses.

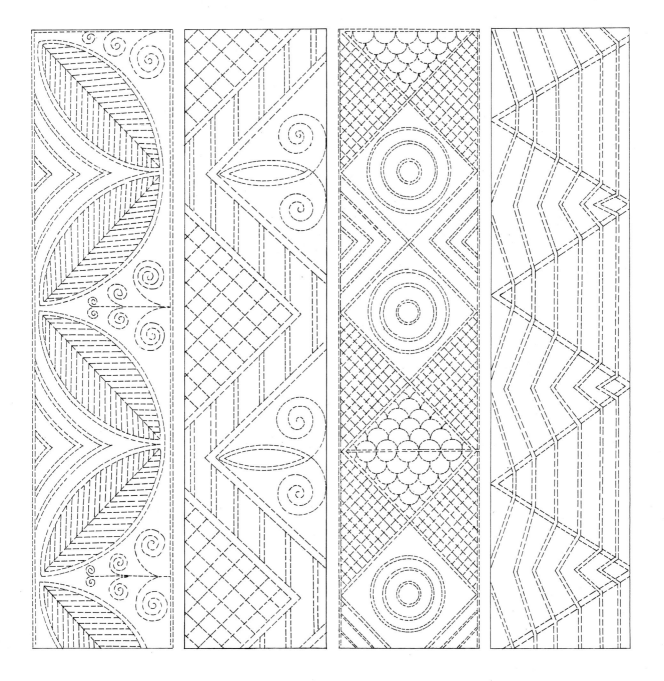

Simple patterns on patchwork and appliquéd quilts

The first two methods described here are used when the quilting pattern is really little more than an echo of the main design. The latter is usually patchwork or appliqué, but these techniques can also be used to highlight the motifs or lines of a strongly patterned fabric.

Outline quilting

A single row of stitches, placed either close to the pieced seams of a patchwork quilt or along the edges of appliquéd patterns, is known as outline quilting. Worked on one or both sides of patchwork or appliquéd shapes, outline quilt stitches are usually sewn about 6mm (¼in) away from the seam or the edge of the shape. Provided you have a good eye, and a measure to check distances, outline quilting can be stitched without marked lines.

When used on pieced and appliquéd quilts, outline quilting provides both the necessary means of holding the layers together and a visual emphasis to the surface design of the quilt. It is the commonest form of quilting found on 'everyday' traditional American quilts.

Contour or echo quilting

Traditionally used on Hawaiian quilts to echo their characteristic appliquéd patterns, contour or echo quilting consists of concentric lines worked around appliquéd shapes or within patchwork pieces. Lines are usually equidistant, but need not be so, provided they remain concentric in form.

Unless the lines are very closely spaced, you should mark the contour outlines on your quilt top before stitching, by hand or machine.

This traditional American pieced block – Turkey Tracks – is outline quilted around the pieced shapes in classic American style.

The appliquéd fish motifs on this sample block by Anne Tuck are echoed with lines of contour quilting, to give texture and interest to the background.

Jan Irvine's unique style of contour quilting is admirably illustrated in this airbrush-dyed silk piece Strike. *The classic but masterly simplicity of the image (photograph by Roger Deckker) is echoed with hand quilting in matching coloured threads. Size: 130cm × 110cm (51in × 43in).*

Quilt-in-the-ditch

The intention behind the technique known as 'quilt-in-the-ditch' is to stitch through the pieced seams of a patchwork quilt, sinking the stitches in the seams in such a way as to make them invisible on the top surface. Quilting 'in the ditch' provides no surface decoration; its purposes are to hold the quilt layers together and at the same time to allow the filling to loft up within the pieced shapes, giving relief and emphasis to the pieced design.

The quilting may be worked by either hand or machine, but machine quilting is much quicker and visually little different to hand quilting. If you use invisible (nylon) thread, this will help to conceal the stitches.

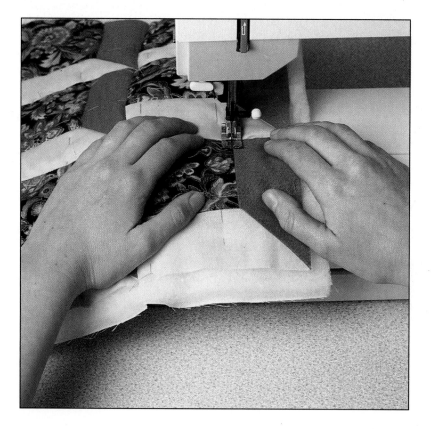

To quilt-in-the-ditch by machine, set the dial for a straight stitch of eight stitches to every 2.5cm (1in). Using your hands to spread the fabric away from the seams, stitch slowly down each pieced seam.

Stitch effects

In contrast to the quilt-in-the-ditch technique, where the aim is that the stitches should not be visible, the stitches form an intrinsic and highly visible part of the pattern in each of the next two methods described.

Meander quilting

Worked by free machining, meander quilting is a wandering line used either as a filling pattern within a quilt design or as an allover pattern across the surface of a pieced or appliquéd quilt. Similar to the vermicelli or crazy stitch of machine embroidery, meander quilting is almost always worked by machine. It is ineffective as a pattern sewn by hand unless a back stitch is used.

Stippled quilting

Unlike meander quilting, stippled quilting is a form of closely-worked filling pattern where no clear lines are apparent; instead, the stitches appear as random depressions on the quilt surface. Stippled quilting is always stitched by hand and is a time-consuming technique, so it is usually only worked as a filler in small areas of pattern.

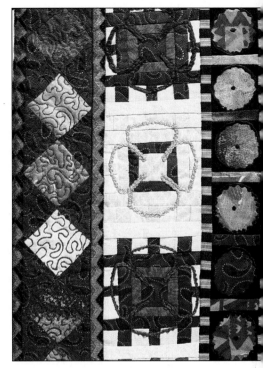

This detail from Barbara Howell's quilt Hashad *shows meander quilting on the pieced squares and triangles, together with other forms of machine quilting.*

In this sample, Wendy Baxter has stipple quilted by hand in a matching thread as a background to highlight the leaf motif on the hand-dyed cotton fabric.

73

Freehand patterns

As well as using freehand drawing to sketch the details inside shapes made with outline templates, you can also draw some complete motifs and border patterns freehand. All too often, though, lack of confidence in drawing skills inhibits experimentation with this kind of pattern. This is sad, because many traditional patterns were drawn in this way by women who not only had no art or design training, but sometimes little formal education either.

Decorative patterns do not require great skill – just determination and practice. Begin by sketching patterns and ideas on paper, and do not be deterred if your early attempts are jerky and weak; confidence and quality of line will come with practice and experience. Once you feel confident with your skills on paper, you are ready to draw patterns directly on fabric, according to the requirements of your design.

Why draw patterns freehand, when templates may be an easier option? Much depends on the style and character of your design, but naturalistic patterns, such as trailing vine borders and baskets of flowers, often have a liveliness and a lack of formality that are more in keeping with their character if they have been drawn in this way. An additional advantage is that it is quicker to draft patterns freehand than to spend time making or buying templates, though you will have to ensure that the quality and character of the design are not compromised. Most importantly, freehand drawing is a sign of self-confidence in your skills and an encouragement towards individual creativity and pattern exploration.

Skilfully-drawn freehand patterns for motifs and borders, and particularly for filling patterns, were one of the hallmarks of the Allendale and Weardale school of quilt designers. Their style is clearly illustrated in the detail of this wholecloth quilt top, marked out around 1900, but never quilted.

FREEHAND PATTERNS

Welsh spiral motifs and border

North Country feather, cockscomb and curlicue

Flower patterns from Amish quilts

Flower pattern from 18th-century English quilt

CHAPTER 4

DESIGN

The most exciting, but perhaps the most exacting, part of quilting or quiltmaking is design. However skilled you become at stitching, the success of your quilts will depend as much on good design as on fine workmanship.

Designing for quilting entails planning which patterns to use on the surface of the quilt, and deciding how to coordinate them. At its simplest, a quilting design can be a single filling pattern used over the whole quilt surface. On the other hand, quilts may be stitched with complex designs incorporating motif, border and filling patterns of variety and intricacy. Between these two extremes, a host of possibilities exists.

So, if the design choice is wide – where do you start? For new and inexperienced quilters, there are advantages to beginning with a traditional design. Simple ways of putting patterns together are just as much a part of the quilting tradition as the patterns themselves. The best traditional design plans are the result of generations of trial and error aimed at achieving balance and proportion, and making each pattern contribute positively to the design. For some experienced and contemporary quilters, though, traditional designs are too conservative and too 'safe' – there is little challenge and too little opportunity to develop individual ideas.

Choosing a quilting design is very personal. Decide which visual patterns or images you like and the ways in which they might be combined; design is as much a skill as sewing and this skill will develop with experience. Be aware, too, that there are practical considerations to quilt design. Quilts are made for a purpose – usually for wall art or bed covers – so they must fit that purpose.

The nature of the surface on which the quilting design will be stitched is another consideration. On any other than a wholecloth quilt in plain fabric, there will be other surface decoration. A pieced or appliquéd cover design may be bold, vigorous and colourful, and could completely overpower subtle, intricate quilting patterns.

The flat planes of this elegant three-dimensional pieced design, Connections, *by Dorle Stern-Straeter (photograph by Patricia Partl), provide space and form for the texture and patterns of a quilting design which she has developed with sympathetic skill. Size: 160cm × 220cm (63in × 87in).*

The intention in this chapter is to take you through these aspects of quilt design, first by looking at the practical considerations, then by explaining the interacting visual elements that relate specifically to quilting design, and finally by showing how to plan your design and transfer it to fabric.

Quilting designs and cover designs

The sandwich of layers on which your quilting design will be first drawn and then stitched has two fabric covers and a batting layer in between. It is usual to refer to one cover as the quilt top and the other as the backing, though this can lead to difficulties if your quilt is to be reversible.

The fabrics used for the quilt top, and the manner in which they are put together, represent the cover design on which the quilting design is superimposed. Quilts (except wholecloth ones or unquilted coverlets) have, therefore, *two* visual designs on their surfaces – the *cover design* and the *quilting design*. The two may be closely coordinated or there may be a deliberate tension between them, but it is important to recognize that they must be considered together for what they are – two visually distinct parts of a whole, in this case a whole quilt.

The balance between the two designs is another personal consideration. If you wish to concentrate on quilting, design your quilt top with space to develop patterns of your choice. If, on the other hand, you want the colour, shape and contrast of patchwork or appliqué to be the most visually striking element of your quilt, with quilting used chiefly for its textural qualities, then design accordingly.

Quilts tend to be categorized according to the design of the top because this is usually the more visually striking. One result of this is that the vocabulary of quilting is based largely on cover rather than quilting designs.

Wholecloth quilts

A wholecloth quilt is one where the top cover is made from only one fabric. Although printed fabrics are sometimes used for wholecloth quilts, solid colours – especially white – have always been more popular, because a clean, pure surface shows the quilting design to perfection.

The fabric for a wholecloth quilt is all-important – the colour, fibre and lustre that you choose will dictate its essential character. Suitable fabric types include dressweight and lightweight furnishing cottons, cotton sateen, poplin, fine wool and silk. Fabrics with a sheen – satin or polished cotton, for example – are widely used, but a polished cotton surface can crackle after washing, and most shiny fabrics lose their glossy quality in the wash. If it is necessary to seam the fabric to achieve the required size, *never* have a seam down the centre of the quilt; instead, join panels symmetrically to a central fabric length.

On a wholecloth quilt, the quilting forms the only surface design (unless a patterned fabric is used), so the stitched lines show to perfection – or imperfection, as the case may be! For this reason, designing and making a wholecloth quilt is often considered a test of the quilter's skill.

The all-white wholecloth quilt was traditionally considered the supreme test of the quilter's skill. The close detail of Echoes of the Past *shows the superlative skill of Lilian Hedley's stitching and pattern drafting.*

Strip quilts

These are pieced from long strips of fabric, usually running down but occasionally across the quilt surface. Borders may be added to the pieced strips, as in the Amish bars design.

To make up a strip quilt cover, seam the raw edges of the strips together by hand or by machine, and press open. When machine stitching, sew the seams alternately from top to bottom and then bottom to top, to even out any stretching.

Strip quilts are simple to plan and execute; the nature of the cover design provides the ideal surface for a quilting design of different border patterns – with no difficult corners!

These paper designs for 'strippy' quilts illustrate a variety of interpretations for this classic quilt design.

Stripped Green was designed by the author in traditional style, but quilted in a hoop from end to end. It embodies all the characteristics of a North Country strippy quilt: an odd number of strips in two colours has been quilted in different patterns, but symmetry is maintained by using the same patterns on equivalent strips to either side of the central strip. Size: 223cm × 213cm (90in × 84in).

Patchwork quilts

Patchwork or piecing, in which fabric shapes are sewn together, is an art in itself, providing the opportunity to combine shapes of infinite variety in different ways. Traditional patchwork designs include:

Block designs – shapes are usually joined into square block units
Strip designs – fabric strips are joined then cut into shapes, or shapes are joined into long strips
Medallion designs – borders of patchwork shapes are worked round a central focus
One-patch designs – a single shape is used for the whole quilt top.

Being less structured and more individual, contemporary patchwork is not so easy to define but no less exciting.

Most patchwork is also quilted to give substance and relief to the quilt surface, but the nature of the quilting design will depend greatly on the degree of complexity of the patchwork. On a top consisting entirely of very small fabric pieces, you may find it best either to outline quilt around the shapes or to create a simple design of strong linear definition.

The simpler forms of patchwork, however, lend themselves to more elaborate quilting. Designs with large shapes and simple borders provide space and a structured form for fluid, decorative quilting patterns. Block designs, in which patchwork blocks alternate with single fabric blocks, also provide space for decorative quilting designs. Some of the most exciting new quilts combine contemporary patchwork images with imaginative quilting, linking the pieced shapes, large and small, within the cover design.

If you are planning a hand quilting design for a patchwork cover, consider the area of the pieced seams. You will find it more difficult to stitch across the seams, and keep a constant stitch length, because of the extra bulk from seam allowances.

Before marking out and stitching the quilting design, make up the patchwork top and carefully press the seams open. The quilt top is then ready to be layered or set in a frame.

Using the style and colour influences of Amish quilts, Jenni Harris made this stunning quilt Kites for Alex *for her daughter. Size: 150cm × 208cm (59in × 82in).*

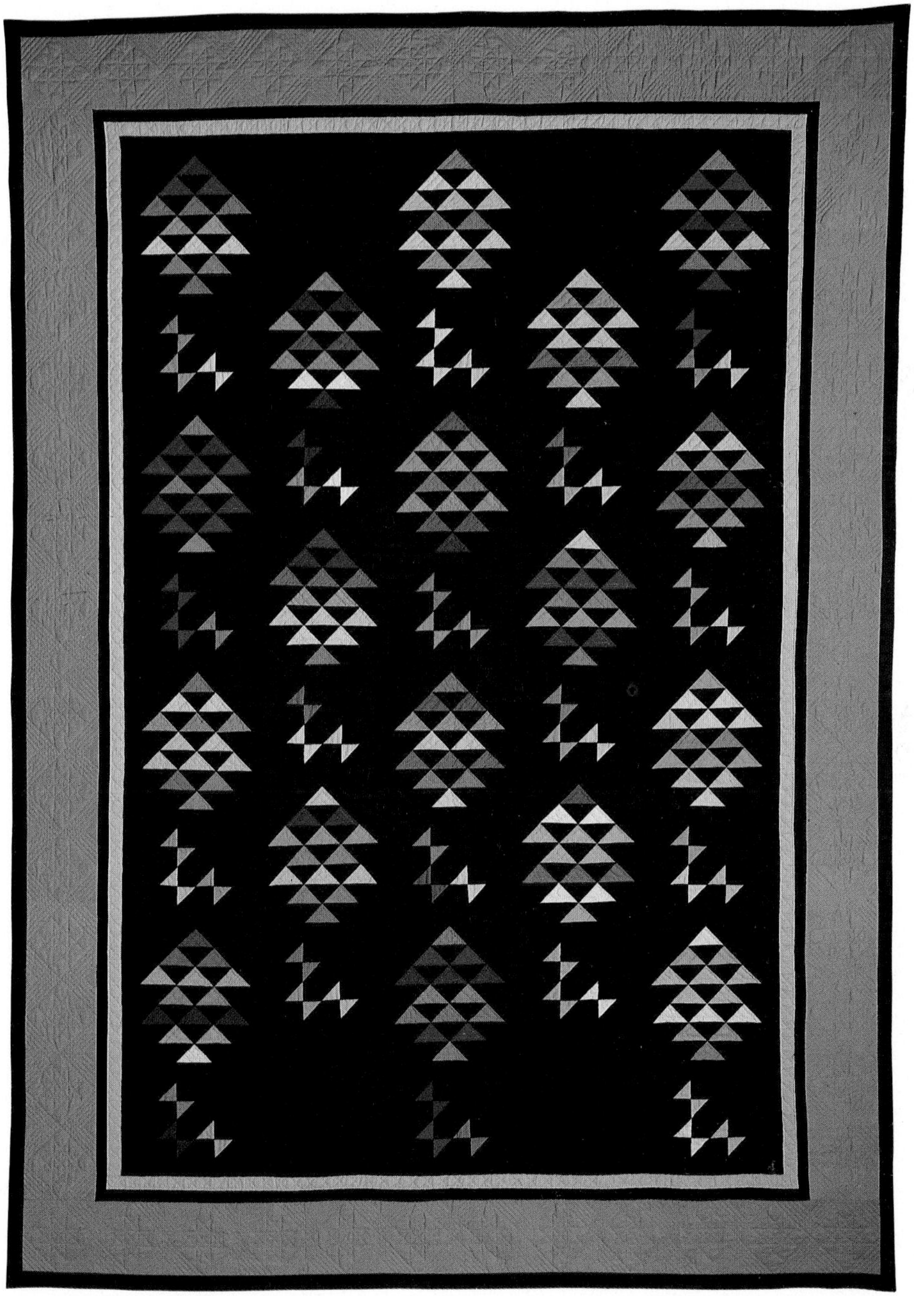

Appliquéd quilts

Sewing fabric shapes on another fabric is the basic form of appliqué. Shapes of whatever kind – pictorial or stylized images, geometric forms, even printed motifs from fabric (a technique known as *broderie perse*) – are cut to size and sewn to a base fabric. The edges of the shapes may be sewn by hand or machine to the base layer. If you are hand sewing, turn in the raw edges and oversew or embroider; if you are machining, use a satin stitch to cover the raw edges – there is no need to turn them in.

Appliquéd covers can be more difficult to quilt by hand than other types of quilt top. This is because the appliqué process leaves two

Painted Metal Ceiling III, *by Anne Oliver, was inspired by the 'endless' tin ceiling of the Woolworth's store in which she once worked. This handsome, ornate and meticulously crafted quilt stole the show at a recent Houston Quilt Festival. Size: 203cm (80in) square. (Photograph courtesy of* Quilting Today.*)*

The close-up detail of Anne Oliver's quilt Painted Metal Ceiling III *reveals her fine hand stitching and careful blending of quilting and appliqué.*

fabric layers on the quilt top rather than one. When batting and lining are added, there will be four layers in any appliquéd areas of a quilt, making it less easy to maintain the same quality and size of stitch here as on sections without appliqué. So if you wish to run your quilting lines over appliquéd shapes, cut out the base fabric inside the shapes, leaving a small seam allowance of about 6mm (¼in).

Traditional quilting design plans

A close look at traditional quilts reveals that the quilting patterns – motifs, borders and filling patterns – fit together in simple but structured frameworks. These well-established design formats, or plans, divide the surface of the quilt into symmetrical spaces within which the chosen patterns are marked. On some traditional quilts, such as the Welsh ones, these spaces are clearly defined within the design by double rows of quilting lines – stitched between central motifs and fillers, and between each of the border patterns, for example. On other quilts, the design spaces are visually clear, but there are no quilting lines to separate the patterns, and this allows a natural flow from one to another.

Traditional design plans provide the beginner with a simple framework into which patterns can be fitted, and encourage both pattern coordination within the symmetry of the design and an understanding of the relationship between the pattern elements.

If you choose a traditional plan, bear in mind the nature of the design on the quilt top. Draw the plan to scale on paper, then sketch in ideas for quilting patterns within the spaces; you will probably try several pattern ideas within the chosen plan before arriving at the most satisfactory one. If you plan a patchwork, appliqué or strip quilt, draw your quilting designs on tracing paper to overlay on the quilt top design.

BORDERED DESIGNS

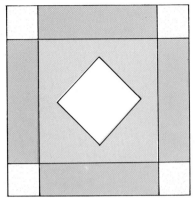 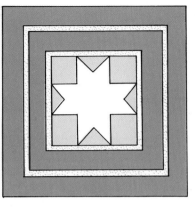 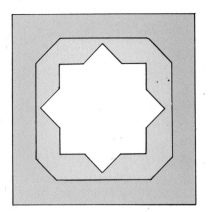

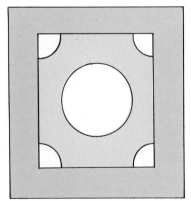 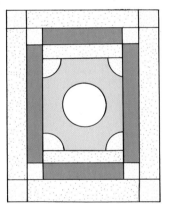 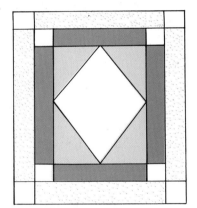

Traditionally, bordered designs have a centre pattern in a centre field surrounded by one or more borders. Corners may be filled with motifs or filling patterns. (These designs represent the arrangement of *quilting* patterns – they are not designs for *pieced* quilt tops.)

STRIP DESIGNS

ALLOVER DESIGNS

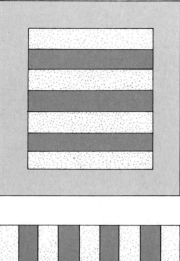

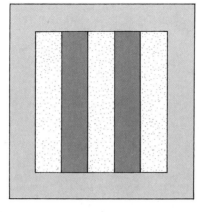

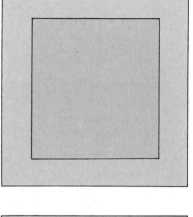

For strip designs, border patterns are worked down or, more rarely, across the quilt; they may have a border frame.

In allover designs a single pattern is worked across the quilt surface, combined, perhaps, with a border frame. Traditional pieced quilts were often quilted in this simple manner.

REINTERPRETING TRADITIONAL DESIGNS

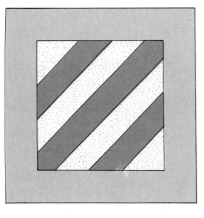 

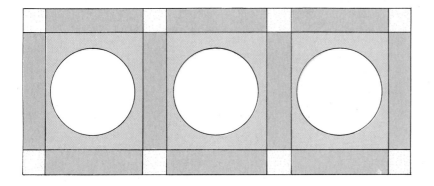

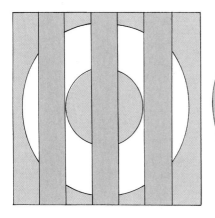 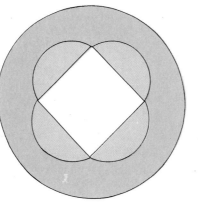

Symmetry and asymmetry

Traditional square or rectangular designs for quilts usually have a basic four-fold symmetry, that is two imaginary lines can be drawn across the quilt surface, dividing it into quarters. Each quarter contains the same arrangement of patterns in the form of a mirror image of the adjacent quarters. Quilts can also have a two-fold or bilateral symmetry, with one half of the design a mirror image of the other half.

Within the overall design, the traditional *patterns*, too, are often symmetrical in form – leaf patterns have the bilateral symmetry of nature, flowers may have an additional radial symmetry. A radial symmetry for the organized grouping of pattern motifs is often used as the central focus of a quilt design, with patterns repeated four, six, eight or sixteen times around a central point.

In practice, this makes traditional-style quilts relatively simple to design and mark out. In the case of quilts which have a four-fold symmetry, once you have chosen patterns and worked out how to fit them into one quarter of the quilt, you need only repeat the arrangement in the other three quarters to complete the design.

Symmetrical quilting designs are generally orderly, calm and,

Four-fold symmetry

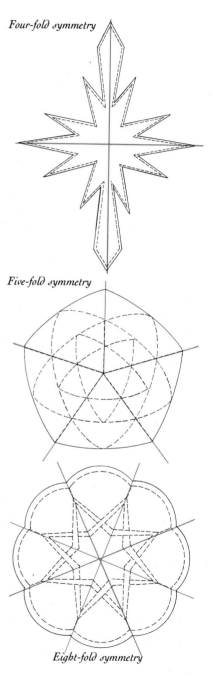

Five-fold symmetry

Two-fold symmetry

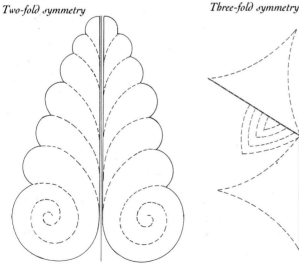

Three-fold symmetry

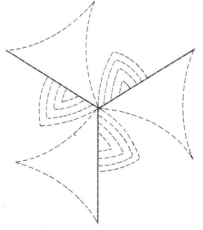

Eight-fold symmetry

when well executed, have a quiet beauty; asymmetrical designs, on the other hand, can bring movement, tension and deliberate disorder in a way that represents a more contemporary design image. With no lines of symmetry across the surface, focal points that may be anywhere on the quilt plane and even, on some quilts, an outline without symmetry or geometrical definition, asymmetrical designs represent a greater challenge.

Space and illusion

An element frequently overlooked, and therefore underused, in quilting design is the importance of space; to consider a space as just another area in which to place a single motif is an all too common mistake in quilting designs.

The various elements within a design can be arranged in such a way that the spaces between them become as important visually as the pattern lines themselves. Because batting fills and raises spaces, they can either become visual foci, or they can provide linear definition within the design, or they can create illusions of shape and form. Examples of all of these uses of space can be seen here.

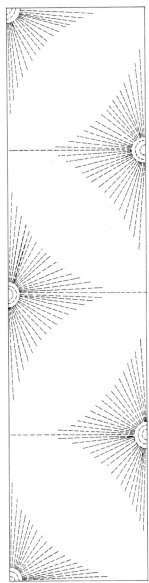

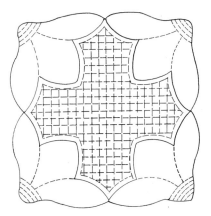

Four flower motifs, symmetrically positioned, leave a cruciform shape as the focus of the pattern.

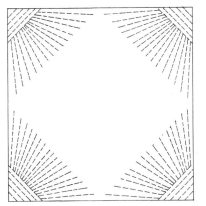

The classic 'diamond-in-the-square' pattern is produced by illusion, as are the curved shapes in the border pattern.

91

Positive and negative

An important ingredient in quilting design is the contrast created within the surface of the quilt. With patchwork and appliqué, colour and shape provide two visual elements for developing contrast, but in quilting the sole means of achieving contrast is to exploit the relationship between the stitched lines.

Where pattern lines are close together, the layer of batting stays firm, dense and relatively flat. Where quilting lines are well separated, batting lofts up in between to create raised patterns. These are the *positive* areas of the design; the densely stitched areas are *negative* ones. These terms are not intended to imply that positive areas are always more important or more visually striking; they simply contrast and stand away from the negative spaces.

Within a design, there may be clear divisions between the positive and negative areas – for example, when positive motif patterns are surrounded by negative filling patterns – but there may equally be a gradation from positive to negative in which quilting lines are progressively stitched closer and closer together.

If the pattern lines are more or less equidistant, the design will contain no positive or negative spaces. This may be intentional in cases where quilting patterns are used for their textural quality. Wholecloth quilts, though, need the contrast of positive and negative space to create interest on the surface plane and to prevent the patterns becoming an indistinguishable blur.

The detail of Margaret Durbridge's quilt The Ayes Have It *reveals her clever use of motifs and filling patterns to create positive and negative areas of relief and depth.*

In The Ayes Have It, *Margaret Durbridge used motifs inspired by celtic art to produce a bordered quilting design for this cool and calm wholecloth quilt in pure cotton. Size: 135cm × 213cm (53in × 84in).*

Designing to scale

The planning stage of a quilting design usually begins on paper. This gives you the opportunity to work out:

- how to divide the quilt surface into design spaces for patterns
- how to fit patterns accurately into spaces
- how to balance pattern elements
- the relationship between positive and negative areas
- the type of symmetry of the design
- the nature and importance of spaces between patterns.

1 Using a large sheet of plain paper, make a scale drawing of your cover design and then colour it in with pencil, paint or cut fabric shapes and glue them in position.

2 Using tracing paper, pencil and ruler, draw your quilting design to scale. Scaled-down pattern templates will help you to draft some motifs; a rolling ruler is useful for drawing certain filling patterns.

3 Place your quilting design over the cover design in order to gain a visual impression of what the two designs will look like when combined.

Setting your ideas down on paper also allows you to develop them, and to experiment with pattern and space. Like any form of experimentation, mistakes will be made – but mistakes on paper are cheaper, easier to rectify and much less heart-rending than mistakes on fabric!

Your paper design will represent both a visual impression of your finished piece and an accurate plan from which to work out all the important dimensions. Because quilts are, for the most part, large textiles, planning on paper usually entails designing to scale. Choose a scale that has a simple numerical relationship to the size of the finished quilt – quarter, fifth or eighth scale, for example – so that any measurements can easily be translated from one scale to the other.

If you are planning a wholecloth quilt, draw your quilting design on plain white paper, such as cartridge paper. Choose the largest size of paper that you can handle; the smaller the scale, the more difficult it will be to draw motifs. For patterns which require templates, you might find it helpful to make scaled-down templates of your chosen patterns in order to draw them on the paper plan.

For pieced or appliquéd quilts, and for strip quilts, make a scale drawing of your cover design first. Use coloured pencils or paper, or even glued fabric pieces (a personal preference), to block in the colours and shapes of the cover, and then draw your quilting design on a tracing-paper overlay.

Planning a quilting design on paper, however, is a two-dimensional exercise. The third dimension – relief – is difficult to show, but it should not be overlooked, so as you plan you must keep clear in your mind which part of your design will be positive and which negative.

Enlarging scale designs

When you have drawn a design to scale, you may wish to enlarge it in order to trace either the full design or some of the pattern elements on the quilt top. The simplest way to do this is to use an enlarging photocopier to increase the design to the required size.

Your scale design can usually be increased in size by 50 per cent or by any percentage in between. Each enlargement can also be further enlarged. The thicker, bolder lines of the final enlargement are ideal for tracing on fabric.

This technique of scale-drawing and then enlarging is particularly useful for geometric designs and patterns based on circles. It is much easier to draw to scale using compasses than to draw large circles by whatever means is to hand.

For Michelle was made by Brenda Johnstone as a 21st birthday gift for her daughter. In ivory satin, this luxurious and stylish wholecloth quilt was designed in art nouveau style with individually developed border and centre patterns, but the traditional 'basket' filling pattern has been used to complement the art nouveau elements. Size: 224cm × 224cm (90in × 90in).

1 Draft the design on plain white paper, using a pencil, a ruler, and compasses, if required. Go over the pencil lines with a black pen, making them either solid or broken, and then enlarge the design in sections.

2 Using your initial design, make photocopy enlargements of sections until you have a complete set of the required size.

3 The final enlarged design can be used either in a cut and taped form or it can be traced onto another large sheet of paper.

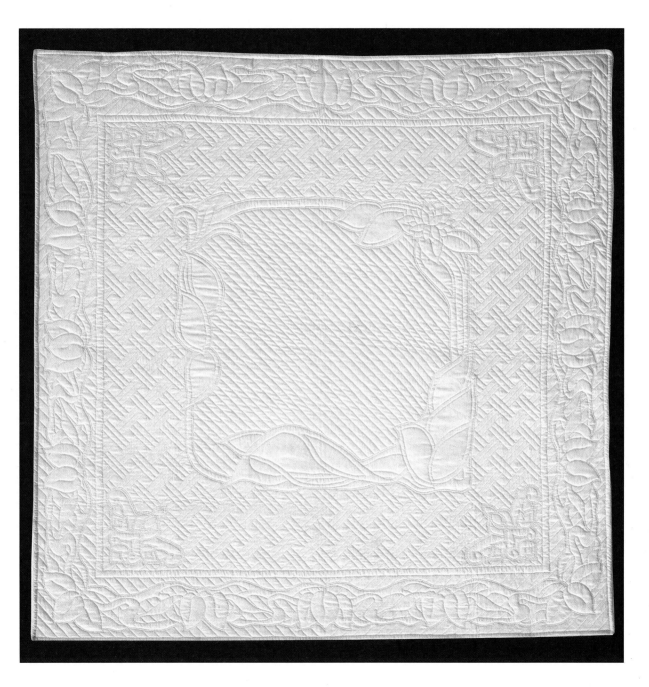

Drafting a full-scale design

You may wish to draft quilting design ideas to the precise size of your intended quilt rather than to scale. You may even decide to do this after preparing a scale design. There are advantages; it gives the clearest possible two-dimensional impression of how the completed design will look on the quilt surface; it allows you to use full-size templates when planning; it gives you a chance to work out how the patterns fit together, and, finally, it provides a completed design which can then be traced on to a quilt top.

You will, however, need table space and large sheets of paper, such as lining paper, if a big quilt is planned. If necessary, piece paper sheets together with masking tape. Remember, though, that if you plan a symmetrical design, only a part of it will need to be fully drafted. For quilts with a four-fold symmetry, only a quarter of the full-scale design is required. If your quilt outline is *square*, the quarter-design can be turned to fit into any of the quarters. For a *rectangular* quilt, however, use either tracing paper or thin paper through which the lines are visible on the reverse. On a rectangle, you will need to turn the quarter-design over to produce a mirror image on adjacent quarters.

Draw out your full-scale design with a hard, sharp, lead pencil, a quilters' ruler and whatever other marking tools are required. Use Blu-tak to anchor your paper to the table top and keep a large eraser close by for the inevitable errors.

If you wish to mark out the quilt top on a light box or glass table, using the pencil-drawn design as a tracing pattern, thicken the pencil lines with a black drawing pen to make them more clearly visible.

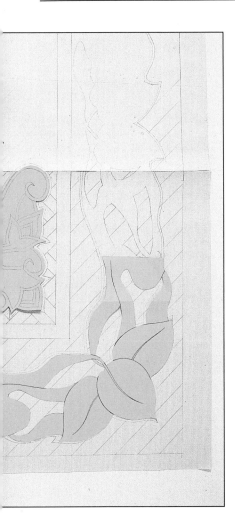

Transferring designs to fabric

More discussion takes place among quilters about the best way in which to transfer quilting designs to fabric than about almost any other stage in quiltmaking. There are two problems to resolve: how to draft the design onto fabric, and which marker to use for the drafting.

The various markers have already been considered (see page 18). To transfer a design to fabric, you can either draw it or trace it – or use a combination of the two.

PREPARATION

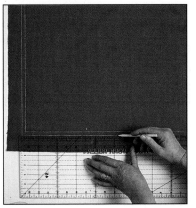

1 Press the quilt top carefully, with all seams open. Set it, right side up, on a table positioned in good light (preferably daylight).

Place the table so that you can work all around it; this will minimize the extent to which you will need to move the quilt top as you mark. Have marking tools and pattern templates close to hand, but not on the marking table – a small trolley alongside is useful for this.

Mark the outer edge of the quilt with either a single or double line – this will not represent the absolute edge of the finished quilt, but the line to which the quilting design will extend. On most quilt designs these outer containing lines are quilted.

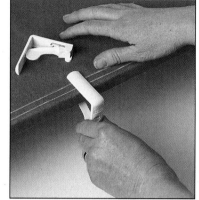

2 Before marking any patterns, mark the important design areas of the quilt, for example border divisions, the quilt centre, and lines dividing the quilt into quarters. If these points and divisions are also lines within the design, use your marking tool to draw them. If not, use basting thread or an easily erasable marker, so that these guidelines can be removed when the design is fully drawn.

3 Anchor the fabric to the table top. If the quilt top is smaller than the table, tape the corners to keep the top in position. If the quilt top is larger, then use clips – for example, table cloth clips – to hold the area you are marking. Fabric is much easier to mark if it is held taut.

Drawing on fabric

Using whatever combination of templates, freehand drawing and line drawing is appropriate for your design, draw directly on the fabric with a marker. To ensure accuracy, check measurements constantly with your paper design as you mark.

ORDER OF DRAWING

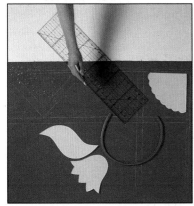

1 Draw motif and border patterns first. To maintain the symmetry of the design, border patterns should be drawn from the centre of the border outwards towards the corners.

2 Once the motifs and borders have been completed, draw the filling patterns. Maintain the accuracy of line width and intersecting angles by constantly checking with a ruler and set square or protractor – most errors are made in marking out filling patterns.

STRIP DESIGNS

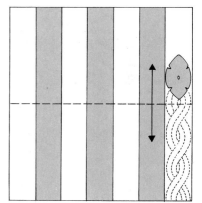

For strip designs which run vertically down the quilt, mark a central *horizontal* line across (with tacking stitches or an erasable marker), and mark your patterns to top and bottom from this horizontal. They should then fit symmetrically into the strip length. Strip designs based on horizontal divisions are similarly marked, but from a central *vertical* line.

Tracing on fabric

Placing pattern templates or a full-scale design under the quilt and tracing the lines is one of the easiest ways of transferring a design to fabric. This cannot easily be done on dark fabrics, however, and you will need either a light box or a glass-topped table with a light source beneath. Small quilts can be marked at a window, but this is quite impractical with a large piece.

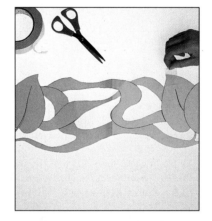
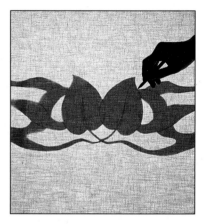

1 Make sure that your basic design or pattern templates have bold, clear lines to follow. Thicken the lines with a black pen if necessary.

2 Anchor the paper design or pattern to the transparent surface with tape, lay the quilt top over the design, positioning it correctly, and secure it. To prevent scorching, keep the fabric away from any unprotected light source.

3 Trace the pattern lines with a marker, following the sequences described for drawing on fabric.

Design pitfalls

Long experience of making quilts and encouraging others to do so has shown that certain common design mistakes are made both by beginners and by more experienced quilters alike. So to give you a helping hand along the road to good design, the following list identifies most of the common problems and mistakes and suggests ways to counter them.

PROBLEM	REMEDY
Finished quilt is flat and patterns do not show in relief.	Use a thicker batting.
Motif patterns are indistinct.	Use two or even three lines of quilting to outline motif patterns (called 'double' or 'triple' lining).
Motif, border and filling patterns 'blur' together with no positive and negative areas.	Create positive and negative areas by using closely-spaced filling patterns between motifs and borders. Use double rows of quilting lines to define spaces, such as border areas, in the design.
Filling patterns are uneven and vary in direction.	Use a set square and ruler, constantly checking the accuracy of line width and intersecting angles.
Design lacks movement.	Combine curvilinear with straight line patterns for interest and movement.
Design looks dull.	Use a greater variety of patterns.
Patterns are isolated and lack coordination.	Arrange motifs in organized groups rather than using them as isolated single patterns.
Patterns do not fit in spaces.	Measure the spaces and the pattern repeats and make sure the pattern repeats fit accurately in the spaces.

CHAPTER 5

SPECIAL EFFECTS

Using patterned fabric

Fabrics with printed patterns, especially cotton prints, have been incorporated within pieced and appliquéd quilts since they were first produced. But while quilters make extensive use of patterned fabrics for pieced and appliquéd quilts, there is a reluctance to use patterned fabrics for wholecloth and strippy quilts, or indeed for any type of quilt where large areas of individual fabrics are to be extensively quilted.

Patterned fabrics certainly present problems, but if you use care and judgement to balance the character of the quilting design with the nature of the fabric, prints can give an added textural quality to any type of quilt. As a general rule, simple geometric quilting patterns will be most visible and will conflict least with large-scale prints. On a smaller scale print, border or filling patterns with continuous and simple line movement are usually most effective; isolated motifs or complex line patterns of any kind generally show less well. Many patterned fabrics – not just stripes and checks – have some form of linear definition; this can be enhanced with a sympathetic quilting design.

As a general rule, you should not use a thin batting if there are to be large areas of patterned fabric within a quilt. The quilting design will be more visible if a substantial batting is used – certainly no thinner than a good quality 56g (2oz) if you are hand quilting and thicker for machine quilting. The heavier the batting, the more strongly sculptured the appearance of the quilt.

On her wild and exotic quilt Green Piece, *Doreen Daniel has subtly used a variety of hand and machine quilting techniques to embolden and decorate the patterns of the fabric. She has machine quilted around animal and plant motifs; hand quilted to continue fabric patterns across pieced shapes or to emphasize leaves and flowers, and used decorative machine stitching to create surface highlights. (Photograph courtesy of the Tyne and Wear Museum Service.)*

To stitch this filling pattern on her quilt Stripped Green, *the author simply followed the lines of the fabric design without any need for marking.*

Texturing and colouring fabric

Inexpensive household equipment is all that is required for fabric dyeing.

Despite the wide range of fabrics available, it is sometimes preferable to add further colour or surface interest to a base fabric before it is quilted. In this way, you can create fabrics that are uniquely individual or that give you the precise colours and tones required for a particular design.

Dyeing and painting are two ways of colouring and texturing fabric, but paint is added to the surface of the fabric whereas dye penetrates through the fibres. Both are very straightforward processes, using easily available and inexpensive equipment – and involve no mystery or magical skill, just simple chemical processes.

To produce mottled effects, as seen on these hand-dyed fabrics by Penny Roberts, is exciting – but unpredictable!

When Ruth Reed chooses fabrics for her quilts, she likes to have several different tones of each colour. She hand dyes cotton calico (American muslin) in her garage to produce beautiful colour ranges such as these.

Dyeing

Fabrics can be dyed to produce a uniform colour throughout or to achieve marbled, mottled or tie-dyed effects. Natural fibres are generally easiest to dye, though some synthetic fabrics dye well. Unbleached cotton calico (muslin) is an ideal fabric to choose if you are a beginner. Silk also dyes well, absorbing colour readily to produce deep, lustrous tones. Wash fabrics *thoroughly*; unbleached calico (muslin) should be given a very hot wash to remove all dressing. If a uniform dye is required, soak your fabric for 24 hours before dyeing.

Use Procion reactive dyes. With a basic set of eight colours – the three primary colours, red, blue and yellow, together with black, brown, white, green and rust – it is possible to mix a very wide range of colours, each of which can then be diluted to give up to eight tones.

Prepare the liquid dye concentrate by dissolving dye powder in hot water (except for yellow, which dissolves more easily in cold water). Precise quantities of dye powder and water will depend upon the colour you wish to achieve and the amount of fabric to be dyed. Add hand-hot water to the bucket(s) and half a cup of salt per gallon of water; stir to dissolve. Add the dye concentrate and stir again (very thoroughly for uniform dyeing, less carefully for mottling and marbling).

To achieve a uniform dye, gently squeeze excess water from the soaked fabric before placing it in the bucket. Using your gloved hands, work the solution into the fabric, making sure that it is completely submerged and evenly spread out. Stir the bucket *every 10 minutes* by hand.

After thirty minutes, add a solution of washing soda (or soda ash) – one cup of soda to eight cups of hot water. Leave the fabric in the dye bucket for a further hour (stirring every 10 minutes), then rinse it thoroughly in warm water to remove excess dye. Finally, wash the dyed fabric with hot water and detergent, preferably by machine.

To achieve mottled or marbled fabrics, or tie-dyed effects, follow the same technique but do not mix the dye colours quite so carefully; use *dry* fabric, dampened in places, and do not stir so frequently. Bunch, pleat and tie the fabric for tie-dyeing. Fabrics dyed in this way should be colourfast and therefore washable.

Painting

Painting, using a variety of techniques and specially-formulated fabric paints, is an increasingly popular method of adding colour and texture to fabrics. Most fabric paints include manufacturer's instructions – follow these carefully, because methods of drying and fixing vary according to the type of paint and formulation used. The applied paint must be fixed if fabrics are to be washable; most paints are fixed when dry by ironing with a hot iron, but some need to be steamed – a more complex process.

Any kind of fabric can be painted, but natural fibres are easiest to begin with. For silk, use special silk paints. Before painting, wash all fabrics thoroughly to remove any dressing. Use dry fabric if you want the painted areas to remain distinct; wet the fabric if you want colours to merge.

Because paint is a surface application, it can increase the density of the fabric, especially when used undiluted, making it more difficult to hand quilt. This applies particularly to stencilled designs, but trapunto quilting to raise the motifs in relief is a popular and successful quilting technique for such areas.

The techniques described for fabric painting are shown here on a small scale, for clarity, but if you adapt your equipment to suit the scale, they can equally be used for long lengths of fabric. For example, you may simply need to use larger brushes, sponges or sprays. Always protect your working surface with plastic sheeting.

STENCILLING

Tape the stencil to dry fabric with masking tape and keep the fabric firmly in position. Using a special stencil brush or artist's paintbrush, dab the paint evenly within the areas to be painted. Use a separate dry brush for each colour. Allow the fabric to dry slowly and thoroughly before fixing it.

SPRAY PAINTING

Use either wet or dry fabric. A plastic atomizer spray can substitute for an air brush. Paint may be diluted with water to produce softer colours; several colours can be over-sprayed to create a spotted or mottled fabric. Dry thoroughly, and then fix.

SILK PAINTING/DYEING

Use commercially-available silk dyes, which can be applied with a household brush on wet fabric. Mottled effects are produced by sprinkling coarse salt over the colour immediately after application. Leave fabrics to dry naturally; brush off the salt, and fix the dye with a hot, dry iron.

SPONGING

Use a clean, dry sponge: cosmetic sponges give the smoothest application. Paint can be diluted with water to give a lighter colour. Begin in one corner of the fabric and work evenly across, pressing the sponge firmly into the fabric to apply dilute solutions, or lightly sponging more concentrated paint.

Sashiko quilting

A simple but distinctive type of hand quilting is the Japanese variation known as sashiko, originally designed to add strength and warmth to working clothes, but now used for decoration on garments and quilts.

The techniques of preparation and stitching for sashiko quilting are the same as those already described for other forms of hand quilting. It is the characteristic patterns, the manner in which they are used, and the bold, highly visible stitches which give sashiko its particular style. The patterns are chiefly geometric grid designs of surprising variety; some are common decorative themes from various world cultures and can also be found on Western quilts. They are stitched with a coarse thread in a colour that *contrasts* with that of the fabric and with running stitches larger than is usual for traditional Western quilting – about 2 per centimetre (4–5 to the inch).

Sashiko quilted pieces usually contain no filling, though a thin filling, perhaps a cotton one, can be added to give weight if required. Fabrics should be firm but not too coarse – fine wool, heavy dressweight cotton or light furnishing cotton are among the possible choices. Use a thread appropriate to the fabric; cotton perlé, coton à broder or even fine crochet cotton are suitable for most cotton and wool fabrics, but silk thread is firmer on silk or crêpe de chine. A no. 6 or 7 between needle will be needed for these coarser threads.

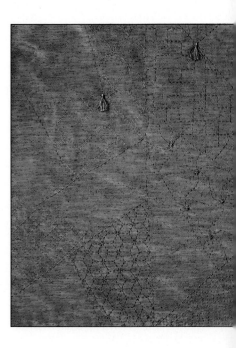

The detail from the back of Margaret Blakeley's polyester-silk jacket shows sashiko patterns in silk threads of various colours, together with beads and tassels for further decoration.

*In classic Japanese style, this jacket
by Margaret Blakeley is hand
quilted with traditional sashiko
patterns, using jade coton à broder.*

Quilting with coloured, metallic and transparent threads

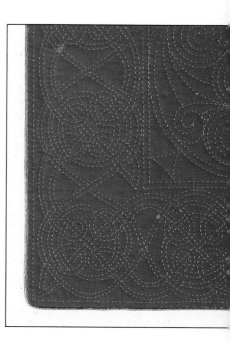

With the exception of Japanese sashiko, quilting in the past has not sought to make the quilt stitch itself highly visible – the line was the important visual element, not the stitches that formed the line. Threads were chosen to match the colour of the fabric and sink invisibly into the surface. On pieced or appliquéd quilts, or any quilt where more than one fabric was used, either a single thread of a neutral colour was chosen or each fabric was stitched with a matching thread.

With a growing range of threads made from natural and synthetic fibres, many of which are suitable for quilting, new and exciting possibilities have opened up, and the stitching can now be a more visible and decorative part of the quilt surface. Experiment with these on sample pieces first to see what effects you can create; take different fabrics, and try various patterns, stitches and thread combinations, then use your imagination to apply the effects you like best to a chosen design.

Coloured threads   Threads in a single colour look stunning when used in a contrasting colour to the fabric of the quilt. In general, the effect is stronger when a dark thread is used on a light fabric – dark thread on a white or cream fabric, for example, or brown on beige.

Variegated coloured threads   Available in various colour combinations, these rayon threads are dyed in a sequence of different colours along their length. When used for decorative machine stitching, especially for satin stitch or similar forms of closely worked swing stitches, they produce bands of changing colour along the line. It can also be interesting to combine a variegated thread in the bobbin of the machine with transparent thread on the top. When this combination is used on a dark fabric surface, the variegated colours show in a subtle, broken form.

Metallic threads   These can produce wonderful shimmering effects on quilt surfaces. For hand quilting, plain gold or silver threads are best and are available in a suitable thickness. For machine stitching,

On Celtic Comforter, *a reversible wholecloth quilt, Margaret Durbridge has used metallic gold thread to stitch her design of celtic-inspired motif and border patterns. The close-up detail (left) reveals her careful designing to carry the border pattern around the corner, the gold-piped edge adding a finishing touch. Size: 74cm × 109cm (29in × 43in).*

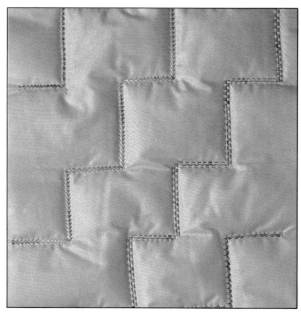

try the thinner variegated metallic threads, which are available in various colour combinations. Use your machine's range of decorative stitches to explore their potential for surface decoration.

Decorative machine stitches in variegated rayon and metallic threads were used to quilt these samplers.

Transparent thread This type of synthetic thread is not intended to show – quite the opposite. It is used to make the stitching line invisible on the top surface when quilting 'in the ditch'. It is also recommended for machine quilting when the intention is to simulate the appearance of hand quilting. The technique is to put coloured thread in the bobbin and transparent thread on top; with this combination, the small coloured stitches formed by the bobbin thread appear on the surface as a broken line, rather like a line of running stitches. The stitching line is still hard and depressed, however, as with any type of machine stitching, so the simulation is only partially successful.

If you are using transparent thread, choose a fine variety from a specialist supplier. The thread available from general haberdashers is usually too coarse.

Cord quilting

Both cord and trapunto quilting, described overleaf, are sometimes called 'Italian' quilting, so to avoid confusion it is better to stick to their specific names. They are decorative forms of stitching in which two layers of fabric are sewn together along the lines of a quilted design and padding of some kind inserted *after* stitching, from the back of the work, in contrast to the 'sandwich' layer of batting stitched into a batted quilt. The stitching can be worked by hand or by machine.

In cord quilting, a design of curved or straight channels is marked on the top layer of fabric and then stitched. After this, special quilting wool or cotton yarn is threaded through the channels. It was a highly fashionable form of quilting on clothes and quilts in the 17th and 18th centuries, professionally worked, particularly in Italy, in elaborate and exquisite designs.

Traditionally backstitched on fine white linen, cord quilting designs are particularly suited to machine stitching. The width of channel will vary according to the thickness of wool or yarn used. With very fine yarn, it is possible to use a 0.4mm twin needle for machine stitching.

Fabrics

Though plain fabrics are usually chosen for cord quilting, striped fabrics can be used to good effect, the channels following the stripes. Fabrics for cord quilting must not be too heavy, or the cord will not rise up on the surface.

The backing fabric must be either of the same weight or heavier than the top fabric to prevent the cord showing more in relief on the back than the front of the work. You will find that it is easier to insert the cord if the backing fabric is loosely woven.

Shadow quilting

In this variation, coloured wools are inserted into the stitched channels and a transparent fabric, such as fine muslin, is chosen for the top. As a result the wool colours show in delicate muted tones, producing an effect similar to that of shadow embroidery.

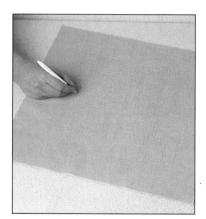 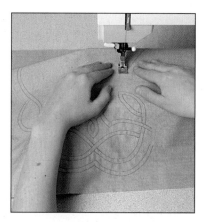 

1 Cut two fabric pieces to the required size (allowing for seams and shrinkage). Mark out the design on the right side of the top fabric, making sure that, at any point where two sets of channels intersect, one set crosses over the other and so forms a continuous channel. If machine sewing, mark the design boldly. The width of the channel should be equal to the thickness of wool or yarn used.

2 Stitch the two fabric layers together along the sewing lines with a machine-sewn straight stitch or a hand-sewn back stitch. You should start and stop in the usual manner, but it helps to have chosen a design which minimizes the need for this.

3 Thread the wool or yarn into a darning needle or bodkin. On the backing fabric, at one end of the channel, ease apart the fabric threads and insert the bodkin, pushing it along the channel either to the end, or to a corner or tight curve. Bring the bodkin out of the backing fabric by again easing apart the fabric threads. Leave a little wool or yarn at the beginning and end of each channel – between 6mm and 12mm (¼ and ½in), depending on the thickness used.

On Desolara *(photographed by Richard Hookway)*, Rita Humphry has echoed the unique shape of the piece with cord quilting stitched in metallic thread to complement the colours of the central design. This is pieced in silks in her characteristic style. Size: 43cm × 102cm (17in × 40in).

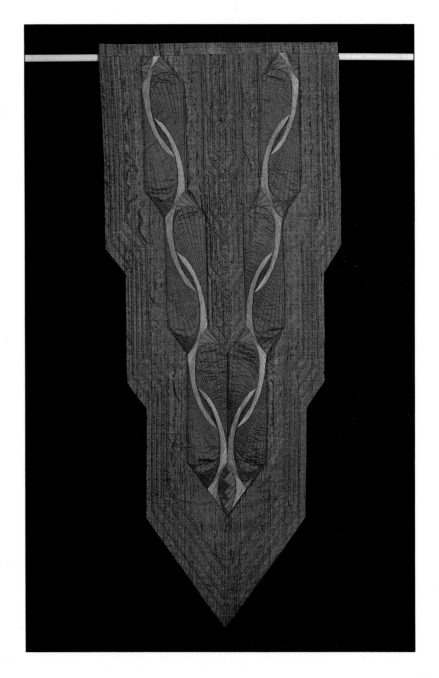

4 To continue along a corner or tight curve, reinsert the bodkin in the same place and carry along the channel line, but leave a small loop of wool at the point of re-entry.

When all channels are cord quilted, a final backing fabric can be added to neaten the work.

Trapunto quilting

The technique of padding whole areas of pattern by inserting loose batting from the back in between the lines of stitching is known as trapunto or stuffed quilting. Both hand or machine stitching can be used, according to choice, but any hand-stitched lines must be very closely worked, either in running stitch or back stitch.

Trapunto quilting can be worked on plain fabric; alternatively, the pattern motifs of a printed fabric can be stitched around and padded to raise their profiles on the quilt surface; flower and animal patterns, for example, can be most effectively padded in this way. Trapunto is also used to pad appliquéd shapes.

The trapunto quilted ring forms of Cup and Ring *by Helen Parrott contribute to the ethereal quality of this machine-quilted and hand-painted silk quilt, inspired by prehistoric stone carvings. Size: 91cm × 152cm (36in × 60in).*

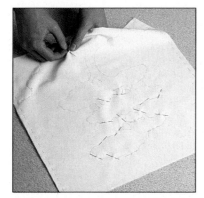

1 Assemble two layers of fabric, as for cord quilting. If you are quilting by hand, the design should be marked on the top fabric, but you should mark backing fabric for machine quilting. Stitch along the pattern lines.

2 Using a fine crochet hook, insert the filling a little at a time through the backing fabric, either by parting the fibres carefully (in small areas) or by cutting a small slit (on larger areas). Use enough filling to create an even raised pattern, but do not overpad the fabric, stretching it.

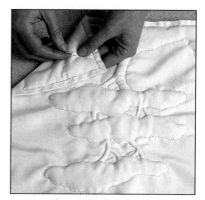

3 To close the holes used for padding, ease back the fibres over holes or close slits with small overstitches. As with cord quilting, a final backing fabric can be added to neaten the work.

Art quilts

It was in the 1970s that a new gallery spotlight shone on quilts and they were exhibited, like paintings, on the walls of prestigious art galleries, particularly in the United States. At first, it was the finest traditional quilts from both public and private collections that were elevated to gallery status and placed in this new context, but perceptions of quilts as works of art, rather than mere domestic decoration, provided the stimulus for a new breed of contemporary artist to use quiltmaking as an artistic medium.

The results of this movement of quilts from beds to walls were twofold: firstly, traditional quilts came to be seen in a new light, a growing and sophisticated audience viewing them as an important art form with strong links to contemporary painting; secondly, trained artists responded to the opportunities that this particular textile medium offered for personal expression. Their understanding of design and form, allied to training and experience, gave them the confidence to challenge the unwritten rules of what had been an orderly traditional craft.

The art quilt movement has put renewed vigour into quiltmaking as a whole. Contemporary quilters have sought to extent the boundaries of the craft, to explore new ideas and techniques while retaining the best traditions of the quilt as a decorative, tactile object of beauty. Each quilt artist has sought to bring a personal stamp to his or her work by developing an individual style and by exploring particular design themes. At the same time, the basic techniques of patchwork, appliqué and quilting remain an essential element, though the degree to which this is so varies according to the style and intent of the quilter.

The art quilts in these final pages represent the work of acclaimed quilters, all of whom use the line stitchery of quilting as a significant element of their work. They are here to inspire, to represent the style of the age and the achievements of this broad-based textile medium. But they also represent a challenge to all quilters to respond to this new era of quilting and take their needle skills outside the domestic setting.

Pauline Burbidge, one of Britain's most highly respected quilt artists, produced Kate's Vase II *as a still-life study in fabric. Using repeated collage blocks of cotton fabrics, some of which she hand-dyed, Pauline then finished her quilt in characteristic style by machine quilting with a simple wave filling pattern, using a multineedle industrial machine. Size: 163cm × 170cm (64in × 67in). (Photograph by Keith Tidball.)*

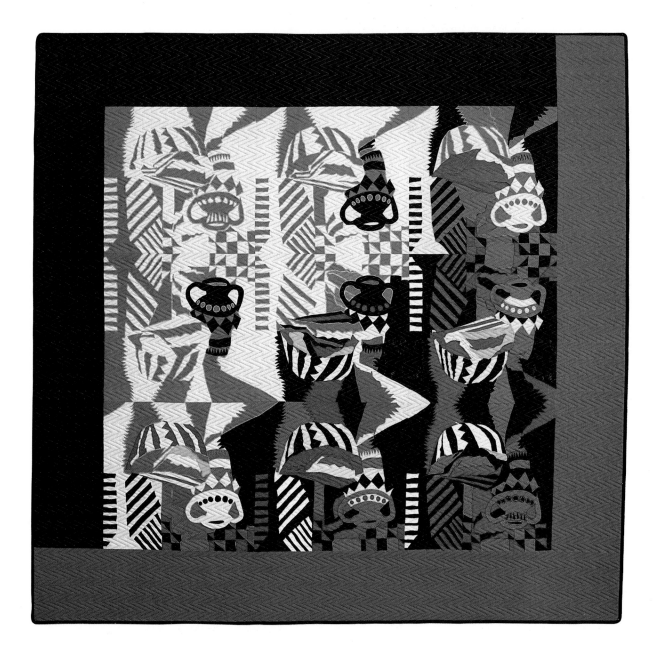

In Broken Heart Quilt, *Charlotte Yde of Denmark has skilfully blended her hand-quilted design with the asymmetrical patchwork design. The variety of quilting patterns and the way in which they are used on this cotton quilt create a work of sophistication and charm. Size: 112cm × 135cm (44in × 53in).*

Drawing on her long-standing interest in, and knowledge of, British landscape and prehistory, Helen Parrott used a variety of techniques to create her elemental quilt Castlerigg Stone Circle. *She screen-printed and hand-painted cotton calico, and used both machine and hand quilting on the thickly padded quilt surface. Size: 152cm × 152cm (60in × 60in).*

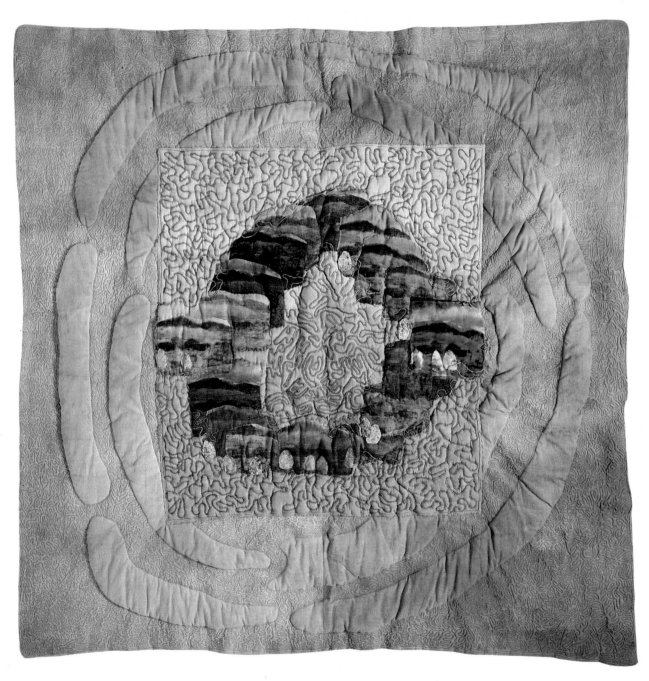

Australian quilt artist Jan Irvine has developed a unique style in which quilting plays a very significant part. In this evocative quilt Caressing the Land, *she has airbrush-dyed silk with a painterly landscape image. Colour and shape within the image are echoed and emphasized with hand quilting worked in contour lines, using matching threads. Size: 160cm × 110cm (63in × 43in). (Photograph by Roger Deckker.)*

Letter to Milano, *by German quilt artist Dorle Stern-Straeter, is cleverly constructed from crazy patchwork triangles to simulate an envelope. Using a variety of fabrics for the pieced design, she has hand-quilted the piece in a pattern of irregular wavy lines which are sometimes referred to as 'wrinkle' quilting. Size: 148cm × 106cm (57in × 42in). (Photograph by Patricia Partl.)*

INDEX

ACKNOWLEDGMENTS

I should like to thank all those quilters who have generously allowed their work to be included in this book. I should also like to thank: Pfaff (Britain) Ltd for the loan of a sewing machine; Madeira Threads (UK) Ltd for threads; Crimple Craft of Harrogate for materials and equipment; Quilt Basics of Cheshunt for threads and equipment; Liberty, Regent Street for fabrics; Philippa Abrahams for a quilt frame; and R&R Enterprises of Malvern for tube frames. Special thanks go to Anne Tuck and Wendy Baxter who helped to prepare the samples.

FOR FURTHER INFORMATION

Merehurst is the leading publisher of craft books and has an excellent range of titles to suit all levels. Please send for our free catalogue, stating the title of this book: –

UNITED KINGDOM
Publicity Department
Merehurst Ltd.
Ferry House
51–57 Lacy Road
London SW15 1PR
Tel: 081 780 1177
Fax: 081 780 1714

UNITED STATES OF AMERICA
Sterling Publishing Co. Inc.
387 Park Avenue South
New York NY 10016-8810
USA
Tel: (1) 212 532 7160
Fax: (1) 212 213 2495

AUSTRALIA
J. B. Fairfax Press Pty. Ltd.
80 McLachlan Avenue
Rushcutters Bay
NSW 2011
Tel: (61) 2 361 6366
Fax: (61) 2 360 6262

OTHER TERRITORIES
For further information contact:
Merehurst International Sales Department at *United Kingdom* address